A Bit of Heaven on the Conestoga

by Lois Martin Zook

A Bit of Heaven on the Conestoga

Copyright © 2001

by Lois Martin Zook
RR 1, Box 240
Middleburg, PA 17842

Library of Congress Number: 99-70612
International Standard Book Number: 1-883294-82-7

Published 2001 by
Masthof Press
*219 Mill Road
Morgantown, PA 19543-9701*

Contents

Preface iv
Meet the People in the Conestoga Valley vi

Chapter 1 - Mounted Riders 1
Chapter 2 - No Elysian Dale 5
Chapter 3 - Strange News 7
Chapter 4 - Susanna's Tick 10
Chapter 5 - Thief 14
Chapter 6 - Make The Grike Narrow 21
Chapter 7 - Linsey-Woolsey 25
Chapter 8 - Freedom At Last 30
Chapter 9 - Springless Wagon 35
Chapter 10 - Grandmother's Wooden Bowl 39
Chapter 11 - Smooth As A Well-Worn Wheel 42
Chapter 12 - Mennonite *Mayflower* 46
Chapter 13 - The Tinder Box 51
Chapter 14 - Dumb Dutchman 56
Chapter 15 - Sudden Solitude 60
Chapter 16 - The Boiling Pot 65
Chapter 17 - Den Of Serpents 69
Chapter 18 - The Runaways 74
Chapter 19 - Swift Waters 78
Chapter 20 - Grandmother At A Hearing 84
Chapter 21 - Land Of Milk And Honey 88
Chapter 22 - Germantown 93
Chapter 23 - City Of Brotherly Love 97
Chapter 24 - Magdelena's Lookout 101
Chapter 25 - A Dream Come True 106
Chapter 26 - Worse Than A Locust Plague 110
Chapter 27 - Catherine 113
Chapter 28 - Gone To Hickorytown 119
Chapter 29 - No Grain 125
Chapter 30 - Vengeance 131
Chapter 31 - Whited Sepulcher 135
Chapter 32 - After The Storm 139
Chapter 33 - Strange Powers 142
Chapter 34 - Overcome Evil With Good 147
Chapter 35 - Captive 153
Chapter 36 - This Elysian Dale 155

Bibliography 162

Preface

In 1709, Swiss Anabaptists settled in the Pequea Valley, in what later became Lancaster County, Pennsylvania. They had been driven like animals, first from Switzerland and then from the Palatinate along the southern Rhine, which for years was a battleground between Germany and France. With torrents of fire and blood, papal hierarchy had determined to end their existence forever. Thus, the Anabaptists became a people without a country.

William Penn, a Quaker, had received land in America as an inheritance gift from the Queen of England. He had offered this refuge to the Anabaptists if they would submit to his holy experiment. His experiment gave all men equal right to live peaceably with those of differing creed and nationality.

The Queen of England and Holland Mennonites had been alarmed at the inhumane treatment the Anabaptists were receiving and offered them assistance to sail to America.

Between 1720 and 1740 some of these Anabaptists (also called Mennonites) settled in the Conestoga Valley of present-day Lancaster County. Few records exist today to show their daily life. Not everyone kept a diary; they were fortunate to find even the back of an old calendar on which to write. Few county incidents were recorded. No newspapers existed. News from afar was frequently out of date and inaccurate, as some learned to their dismay. While eking out an existence, the Mennonites had no time to take minutes in church leadership meetings. Today, only a few names and dates can be salvaged here and there, while other details can only be imagined. Someone has said that with so few Bibles and songbooks, there had to be strong leadership and strong families to pass on the faith.

A Bit of Heaven on the Conestoga shows the struggles, trials, fears, and temptations the settlers may have faced. They hardly knew which way to turn; only their adherence to teachings of sound scriptural leadership carried them through.

* * * *

Thanks and appreciation must be expressed to my husband and children for their encouragement, suggestions, and criticisms.

Also, thanks to my English teacher for four years—A. Grace Wenger—who inspired me to appreciate good literature and especially inspired me to write. Without this background, I would never have had considered doing research and weaving in this story.

Memories of the impressionable simple home and lifestyle of a gone by friend of years ago—Elam Groff—helped me to realize that life is so different today.

Thank you also to historian Amos B. Hoover and his wife, Nora, who spent considerable time sharing their knowledge and understanding of the German-thinking community in the 1720s and 1770s.

Appreciation must also be expressed to retired historian Clarence Spohn of the Ephrata Cloister who placed much valuable information at my finger tips, told me where to find other hard-to-find information, and who translated German information into English.

Thanks to John Spicher, Jr., and historian Norman King for helping to find the mechanics of an old clock.

Many other persons encouraged me to complete this book including my mother-in-law, the late Esther Zook, and our aunts, Minnie Good, Mary Yohn, Fannie Zook, Anna Cashwiler, and Barbara Eberly, who can all still see the good amidst the hard things in life.

Finally, it is my parents to whom I wish to express appreciation. My parents—Anna Mary Weaver and the late Luke S. Weaver—both enjoyed history and viewed the land on the Conestoga farmland, their vantage point at the Fairmount Homes Retirement Community, Farmersville, Pennsylvania. They have been a living reminder that Conestoga with its aches and pains is still a wonderful place to live.

- Lois M. Zook
RR 1, Box 240
Middleburg, PA 17842

v

Meet The People
In The Conestoga Valley

1. **Susanna Ulrich** (main character, fictitious)—b. 1714, youngest of four orphaned children of Peter and Catherine Ulrich. Her older (fictitious) siblings were:
    a. Catherine Ulrich, b. ca1708, m. Samuel Eckerlin (see #10)
    b. Peter Ulrich, b. ca1712, m. ___ Hess
    c. Christopher Ulrich, b. ca1713, m. Bright Star (see #19)
2. **Hans Ulrich Huber**—m. Margaret Koch; children:
    a. Jacob Huber (see #3)
    b. Anna Huber (see #4)
    Hans Ulrich Huber was a great-uncle to the Ulrich orphans (see #1) who called Hans and Margaret "Grandfather" and "Grandmother." The Hubers raised the Ulrich children and were some of the earliest Mennonites who settled near New Holland, not far from Mill Creek.
3. **Jacob Huber**—son of Hans Ulrich Huber and Margaret Koch (see #2); children:
    a. Maria Huber, b. 1714, m. Jacob Eberly
    plus five other children (including Catherine, b. 1729)
4. **Anna Huber**—dau. of Hans Ulrich Huber and Margaret Koch (see #2), m. Marx Graf
5. **Hans Graf**—m. 1) Magdelena (see #7) (only name is fictitious); child:
    a. Jacob Graf, b. ca1703 (see #8)
    m. 2) Anna Herr; children:
    b. Peter Graf, b. ca1711, m. Susanna Musselman
    c. Marx Graf, b. 1712, m. Anna Huber (see #4), had three children
    d. Feronica Graf, b. 1714
    e. Samuel Graf
    f. David Graf, m. Susanna Ulrich (see #1)
    g. John Graf
    h. Mary Graf
    i. Hannah Graf
    j. son
    Hans and Anna Graf were the first settlers on Graf's Run. Hans, a Mennonite, arrived in Germantown, Pennsylvania, in the 1690s.

6. **Peter, Marx, Feronica, and David Graf** (see #5)—friends of the Ulrich children (see #1)
7. **Magdelena Graf**—first wife (fictitious) of Hans Graf (see #5)
8. **Jacob Graf**—son of Hans and Magdelena Graf (see #5), married, had three children
9. **Martin Graf**—Mennonite deacon, younger brother of Hans Graf (see #5), married, had three children
10. **Anna (Henderson) Eckerlin**—widow of Michael Eckerlin who died in Europe, later settler whose family were pietists and became Mennonites; children:
    a. Samuel Eckerlin, b. 1703, m. Catherine Ulrich (see #1)
    b. daughter, died at sea
    c. Emanuel Eckerlin
    d. Israel Eckerlin
    e. Gabriel Eckerlin
11. **Veronica Eberly**—widow, later settler; children:
    a. Jacob Eberly
    plus other children, including a son Ulrich, b. 1726
12. **Christian Wenger**—Mennonite minister, brother to Elizabeth Wenger, m. Eve Graybill; child:
    a. Hans Wenger, b. 1731
13. **Alexander Mack**—bishop and founder of the German Baptists
14. **Conrad Beissel**—early settler, minister of the first German Baptist congregation in the Conestoga Valley, began the Settlement of the Solitary (later called Ephrata Cloister)
15. **Peter Miller and Conrad Weiser**—dignitaries who joined Conrad Beissel
16. **Hans Rudolph Nagele**—minister of Graf's Run Mennonites, later joined Beissel
17. **Anna and Maria Eicher**—German Baptist women who followed Beissel, daughters of Daniel Eicher
18. **Christopher Sauer**—m. Marie, later settlers, pietists; child:
    a. son
19. **Quick Foot**—a Mennonite Indian family (fictitious); children:
    a. Bright Star, b. 1714, m. Christopher Ulrich
    b. Seeking Hart, b. 1725
20. **Theodorus Eby family**—early Mennonite settlers
21. **Joel and Jemima**—(fictitious) from whom we learn how slavery was faced in Penn's Woods. It is likely that there were black persons in the area at this time and Mennonites befriended them.

Graf's Run and South

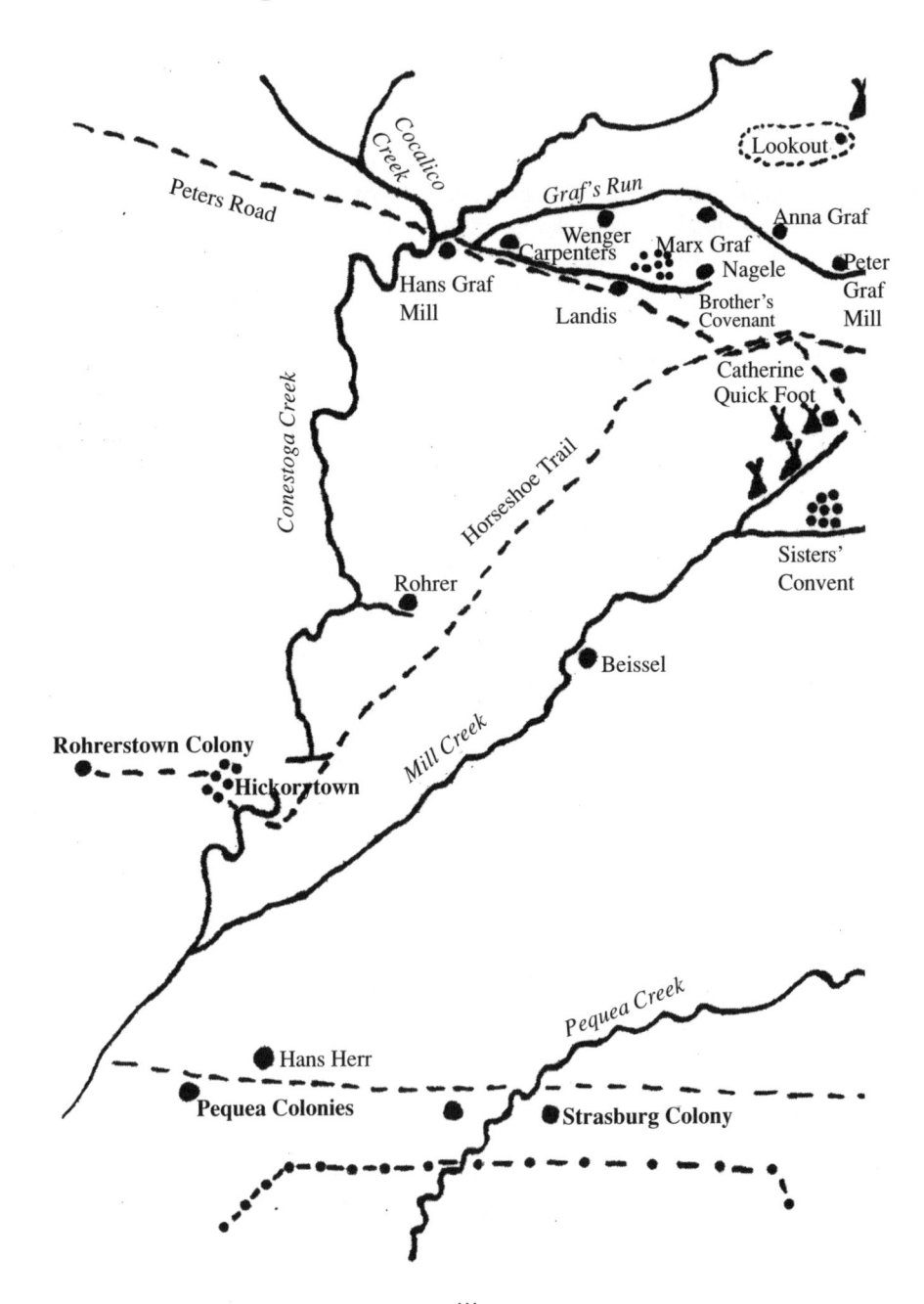

To The Pequea Colonies

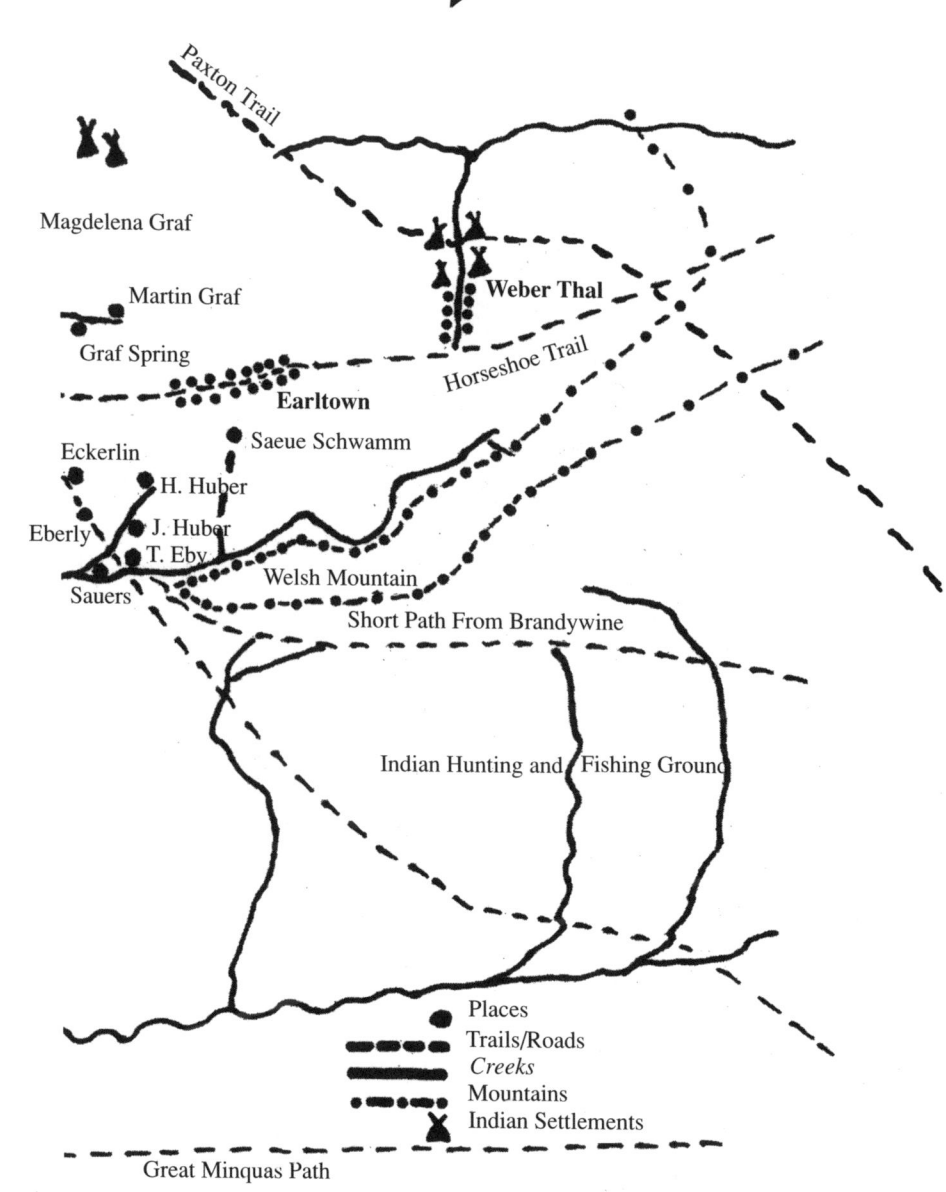

Paxton Trail

Magdelena Graf

Martin Graf

Weber Thal

Graf Spring

Horseshoe Trail

Earltown

Eckerlin

Saeue Schwamm

H. Huber

Eberly

J. Huber

T. Eby

Sauers

Welsh Mountain

Short Path From Brandywine

Indian Hunting and Fishing Ground

- ● Places
- ▬▬▬ Trails/Roads
- ━━━ *Creeks*
- ●●●● Mountains
- ⩜ Indian Settlements

Great Minquas Path

Graf's Run (south) and

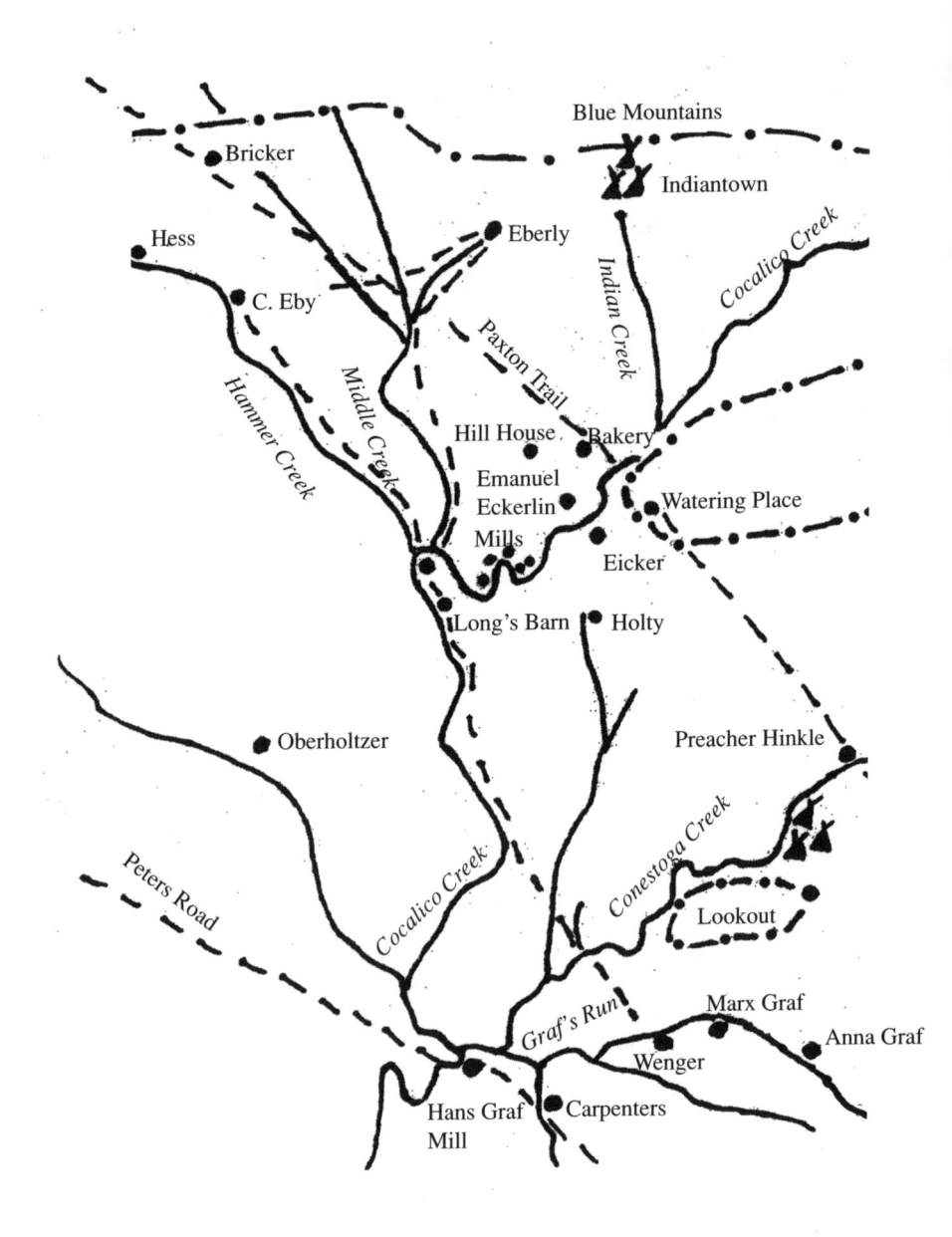

Eberlys Near Indiantown (north)

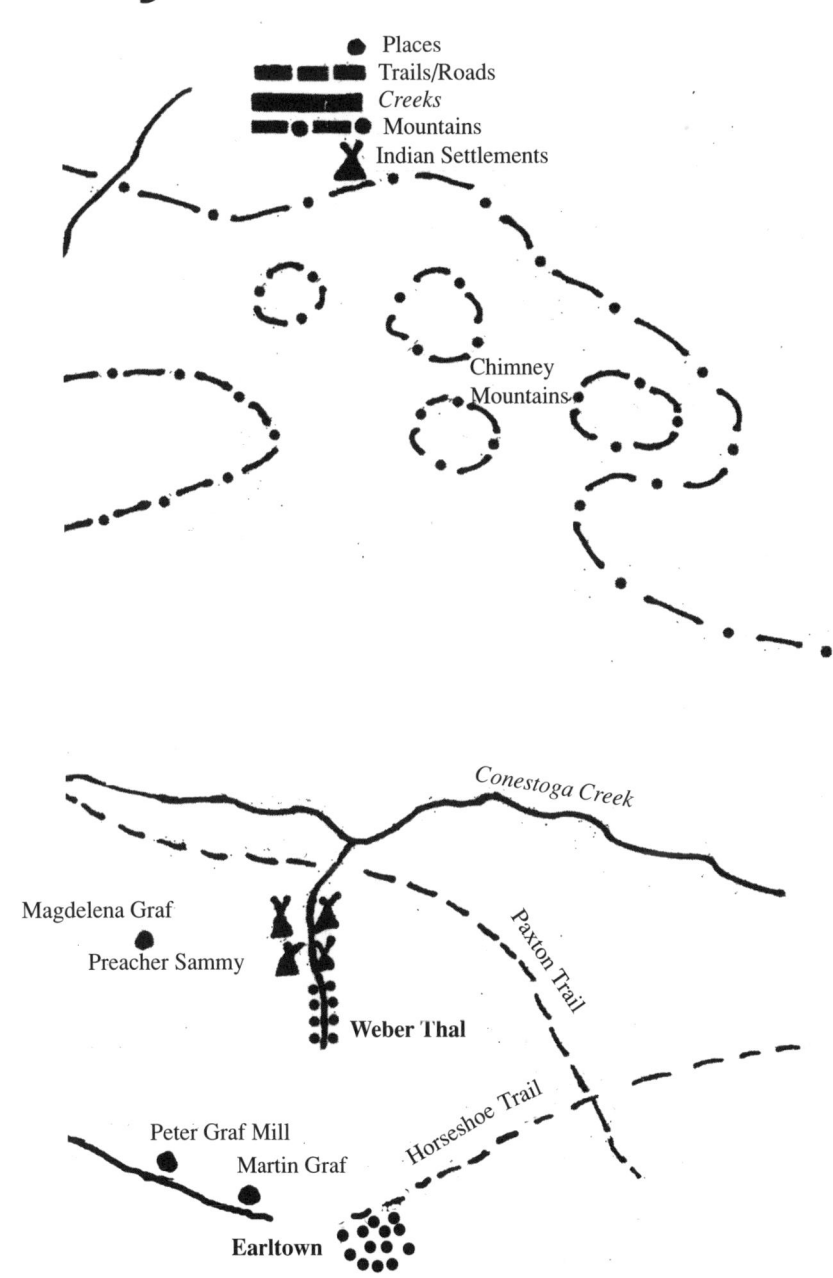

- Places
- Trails/Roads
- *Creeks*
- Mountains
- Indian Settlements

Chimney Mountains

Conestoga Creek

Magdelena Graf
Preacher Sammy

Paxton Trail

Weber Thal

Peter Graf Mill
Martin Graf

Horseshoe Trail

Earltown

xi

Chapter 1

Mounted Riders

Susanna Ulrich glanced down the trail again. She had hoped that at least one traveler would bring some excitement today.

It was November 9, 1724, Susanna's tenth birthday. To make the day special, Grandfather Huber had sent Susanna's older sister, Catherine, and her brothers, Peter and Christopher, along with her to gather walnuts.

The four Ulrich children were orphans who lived with Hans and Margaret Huber in the forest at the end of Saeue Schwamm. Hans was their great-uncle, but the orphans called the Hubers "Grandfather" and "Grandmother." Susanna loved Grandfather and Grandmother dearly. She respected them and was a willing worker. She was happy and carefree, yet serious-minded for a girl of her age.

The Hubers were Anabaptists who knew the pain of separation from family, friends, and possessions. Perils of the sea, sickness, and hunger were familiar with them. Their weather-beaten faces and rough hands spoke of hard toil. Their unfaltering faith in God made them some of Conestoga Valley's most respected persons.

The walnut trees where the Ulrichs were gathering nuts were located on the corner where Peters Road and the Horseshoe Trail joined. Saeue Schwamm was a long strip of grassland which lay centrally between Mill Creek, Graf's Run, and Weber Thal—the southern part of the Conestoga Valley. North of it, in the uninhabited forest, numerous streams emptied into the Conestoga Creek. The Conestoga Valley was the most fertile, well-watered land in Penn's Woods (later called Pennsylvania).

The lowing of cattle in the Schwamm reminded Susanna that evening had come. Suddenly, the Ulrich children heard women's voices, an unusual sound.

"They look like German Baptists," sixteen-year-old Catherine observed aloud as ten women appeared.

2

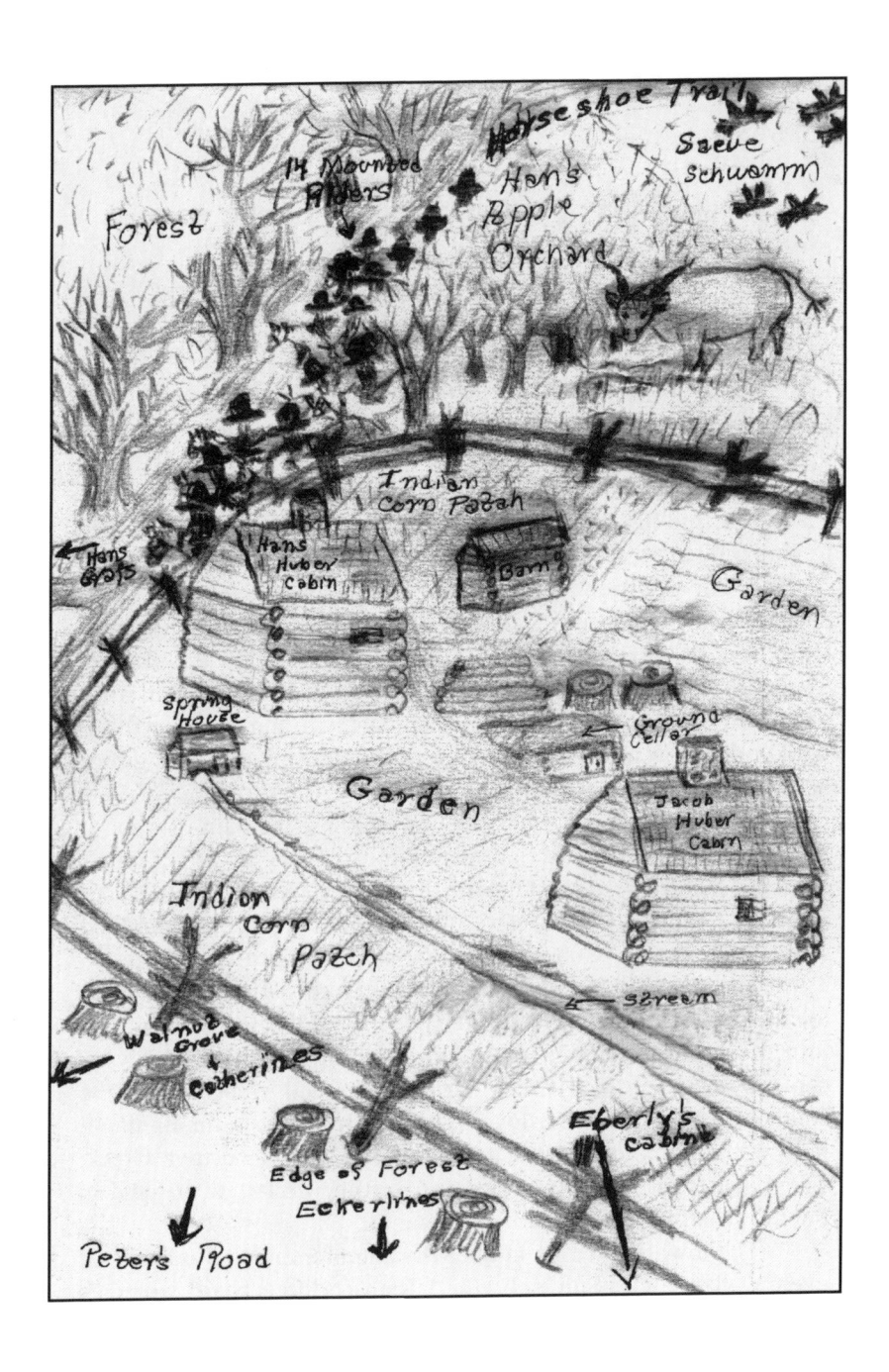

"Sometimes German Baptists bring trouble," Peter spoke suspiciously.

My twelve-year-old brother Peter learns many things from his friend Peter Graf and Peter's father, Hans Graf, Susanna marveled to herself.

"What are so many of their women doing here?" Christopher blurted out.

Christopher's eleven-year record of asking questions, Peter's answers, and Catherine's motherly precautions always gave Susanna much information.

Before Christopher's question could be answered, the group disappeared toward the west. Never before had Susanna seen such a sight.

With their sled full of nuts, the Ulrichs walked toward home.

At the edge of the Schwamm Peter stopped. "What is going on?" he cried.

They heard a distant thumping of hoofs from the far end of the Schwamm.

"It sounds like more horses than the Conestoga Valley's people own," Christopher figured aloud. "Grandfather is fortunate to have one pair of oxen. At the most, Hans Graf has eight horses."

Already Susanna was counting the fourteen mounted riders approaching them. Never before had such intruders broken the silence of their tranquil pasture. Would more riders come? All Susanna knew was an isolated world of peace and quiet. Would her sweet innocence change to bitterness, should troubles come which would leave her people not knowing which way to go? Could a bit of heaven be found amidst heartbreak and tumult?

"More German Baptists are coming!" Peter exclaimed. "They must be coming from Brandywine to have meetings. Those who walked must have taken the shortcut through the Indians' hunting ground."

A lady must have a good reason for an all-day walk along the foot of Welsh Mountain, Christopher was certain. Those deep-rutted Indian trails through the headwaters of many creeks make walking difficult.

"They'll probably have meetings with our neighbors," Peter explained.

One by one each of the horsemen waved and disappeared into the forest.

"They are taking the short path to Hans Grafs. Grafs are Mennonites. They don't want to become German Baptists!" Christopher wanted an explanation.

The next day Peter Graf arrived with exciting news. "Two nights ago the mounted riders slept in Webers' barn in Weber Thal," he exclaimed. "The Webers were friendly, but they were too well grounded in their Mennonite faith to be moved."

"The evangelists have come to arouse any scattered German Baptists and Mennonites who will hear them," Peter Graf explained, emphasizing the last four words. "Last night Mother fed them, and my father slept with them in the barn. This morning he sent them away. I followed them to the home of our minister, Hans Nagele."

"I hope they don't influence the Nageles," Grandfather spoke with concern.

☦   ☦   ☦   ☦

Three days later, Grandfather's son, Jacob Huber, who lived down the trail with his wife and children, took grain to Eby's Mill to be ground, and brought home more news.

"After visiting the Nageles, the evangelists followed Mill Creek to Bird-in-Hand to visit Conrad Beissel," Jacob told them. "They must have used their most persuasive powers on Beissel, because he has experienced a great awakening. Beissel has been baptized by the evangelist's bishop. After his baptism he reminded the bishop that he was only a lowly German whose soul is less pure than his own.

"Through Beissel, the so-called gifts of the Spirit were made manifest. Enough of them were baptized to start regular meetings. In spite of their misgivings, the evangelists ordained Beissel to be the minister of the German Baptists in the Conestoga Valley."

"Beissel might become a great leader," Grandmother suggested.

"Great, but we cannot follow him," Jacob replied. "Beissel's mother and father died and left him an orphan. When he was age twenty-five, he met God and received a vision without help from any man. Five years ago, he came to America to spend the rest of his life alone with God.

"A year later, he and three of his friends settled here. When his turn came to hunt meat for the day, he refused. He said he had not come to fatten the old Adam. Finally, his friends became angry and left."

4

Chapter 2

No Elysian Dale

Beissel quickly gained many followers. Susanna saw him for the first time one afternoon at Eby's Mill. She had expected nothing unusual from the little man. He was of medium build. From the side, his receding hairline revealed a high forehead. His nose was straight and came to a point, which made him look intelligent, she thought.

When Beissel turned to leave, Susanna met him face to face. She felt uncomfortable; his sharp black eyes seemed to look straight through her as if to ask, "Who are you?"

I don't want Beissel to remember me, she resolved. *If he looks at people like that when he preaches, I never wish to be there.*

☩ ☩ ☩ ☩

It was spring. All day Jacob Huber had broken the sod of his newly cleared land. He was tired and welcomed a time to relax and talk with his father. He walked down the trail to his parents' home and greeted his father as he entered the cabin.

"South winds bring rain and we need it," Jacob announced with anticipation.

"Troubles have come to the Conestoga Valley like a storm since last November," Grandfather recalled. He peeled another sliver of wood from the yoke which he was carving for his oxen.

Susanna was at the fireplace, stacking wood she had just brought into the cabin. Her face grew sober. Grandfather seldom talked about problems, but tonight she sensed he would talk.

"If a knife could peel problems away as fast as chips, the Conestoga Valley would be like heaven," Jacob insisted. "Since that day the Conestoga Valley is no longer the elysian dale that its first settler, Hans Graf, declared it to be. The evangelists and Beissel have ended any air of 'home, sweet home' in these parts."

"They were too hasty to ordain Beissel," Grandfather reminded his son. "Already their disappointed followers want to move back to Germantown."

As Susanna's stack of wood beside the fireplace grew higher, Jacob's voice also rose to a higher pitch.

"Beissel's strange doings are going to concern us, too," Jacob exclaimed. "Johannes Landises have invited Beissel to their place for meetings next week. Beissel has been visiting with the Nageles, and the Landises live too near them not to be influenced. Johannes's wife and the Nageles have become attached to Beissel. Johannes does not trust the man."

"The women are so easily deceived, and our minister is confused, also," Jacob's father cried as the creases on his brow deepened.

"Brother Nagele is disturbed about the Mennonites' complacency. Our meetings are too formal," Jacob continued. "Nagele wishes that we would attend Beissel's meetings."

Susanna went outside for another load of wood. She was troubled. *Surely the Landises and Nageles won't leave us. I will miss their children at our meetings.* She gathered the wood and watched Jacob leave. A gust of wind from the schwamm suddenly wrapped her long skirt around her, almost pushing her through the doorway as she entered the cabin.

"What does elysian dale mean?" she asked Grandmother when her arms were empty.

"Elysian means heaven-like," Grandmother replied.

"Jacob says that the Conestoga Valley is not an elysian dale anymore," Susanna told Grandmother.

"For now, the warmth from the fire and smells of a promising supper can be our elysian place," Grandmother assured her.

"Our home is an elysian place," Susanna answered contentedly as she placed the wooden bowls and spoons on the table.

Suddenly, Watch stood to his feet, lifted his nose toward the trail, and left out a long whine.

CHAPTER 3

Strange News

Grandmother and Susanna hurried to the door to see if someone was coming. They saw Christopher and Peter enter the clearing with a load of chestnut fence rails. They, too, stopped to look. Apparently Watch had heard someone coming up Peters Road.

"It couldn't be Hans and Peter Graf," Peter informed them. "On their way home from Germantown, Hans received notice to return. A Quaker friend offered to care for his wagon and horses, and Hans went back. Peter hurried home for Jacob, his oldest brother, and they followed their father. They were to meet a lady whom Martin Kendig had sent from Europe."

"Why would Peter take Jacob to Germantown?" Grandmother asked. "His wife and little ones need him at home."

"It sounds strange. The lady must be very important to need three of the Grafs to meet her way down there!" Grandfather sounded suspicious.

Does Grandfather know something? Susanna wondered. *Who is this lady?*

In her mind Susanna could see Hans Graf leaving his six horses and white wagon. Likely the wagon was stacked high with blankets for the Indians. Under those blankets were tucked many things which Conestoga Valley settlers needed from Germantown. There might be material, needles, knives, paper, iron kettles, salt, and more.

Hans owned more and better horses than anyone else in or near Conestoga Valley. His wagon was the largest. Because Hans was a trader, the Indians traveled down the creeks from far away to trade with him along the Susquehanna River.

Hans refused to trade liquor or knives for bearskins, so the Indians accepted Germantown's woolen blankets.

Usually Quick Foot, an Indian friend, accompanied Hans. They could each speak the other's language well. Sometimes Peter Bezellion, a French trader, traveled with them. The well-known Peters Road was already named for Peter Bezellion before Hans Graf moved to the Conestoga Valley.

The Peters Road began halfway between Philadelphia and Harris Ferry (later called Harrisburg). There it left the Great Minquas Path and went north toward Hickorytown (Lancaster). From there it crossed the Conestoga Creek and followed the Little Conestoga Creek to the Chickies Creek. Passing a place of many springs, it went west to the Susquehanna River and north to Harris Ferry.

At night the traders slept in shelters they had hastily erected near the Indians. The Indians gave them food, and Hans taught them the Word of God.

Susanna's thoughts were interrupted by another whine. Watch knew something was coming, but Susanna still heard nothing.

Hans is at Germantown now, Susanna's mind wandered again. At the thought of Germantown, her thoughts always took a leap. Someday she hoped to see the Germantown Mennonite Meetinghouse and the school where her sister Catherine attended.

Taking a further leap, Susanna's mind took her across the sea to Martin Kendig in Europe.

Earlier news had come telling of the terrible persecutions there. Many of their relatives were being martyred for their faith. Others were fleeing by the thousands down the Rhine River toward Holland, praying that God would provide them a way to Penn's Woods. Many of them would die en route so that others could find freedom.

Conestoga and Pequea church leaders were burdened with the sad news. They had cast lots among themselves to determine who should return to Europe to help their suffering brethren to come. The lot had fallen on Bishop Hans Herr, but he was too old and feeble to cross the sea. Apparently God did not want any of their leaders to go, so they asked for a volunteer; Martin Kendig offered. He, Hans Herr, and Hans Graf had rights to many acres of land where their brethren could settle. Later, if they became citizens, they would work together to pay for it.

Before leaving Europe, Martin, with tears, asked for prayer. He was willing to give his life so that others might come. Grandfather had prayed for Martin every day, and Martin arrived safely.

Watch left out another long whine.

At the first sound of hoofs, Christopher told the Ulrich-Huber household, "It's Benedict Brackbill's horse!"

"And Christian Herr's horse!" Peter added. The Ulrich brothers knew the trot of every horse within thirty miles.

"I wonder why they're coming. No one travels needlessly this time of night," said Grandfather, stating what they all knew. Too many panthers and wolves prowled at night for one's safety.

Eventually the riders came into view and stopped at the cabin. Susanna was happy to see Brother Benedict.

After introductions, arrangements were made for the two visitors to stay for the night and to visit with the Hubers. Grandmother was making a good supper.

Maybe I'll hear more about the news from Europe, Susanna hoped.

CHAPTER 4

Susanna's Tick

A flash of lightning illuminated the Horseshoe Trail which marked the northern edge of Saeue Schwamm. The fast moving clouds meant rain would soon arrive. Before the storm, Susanna was quickly gathering more firewood.

Saeue means pig in the English language, but I never see any pigs there, Susanna mused. She spoke German but was learning some English also.

On nice days, Susanna loved to roam the secluded trail, which wound around rocks and fallen trees. Colorful mushrooms and lichens peeked from the rotted wood. Moss, ferns, jack-in-the-pulpit, and skunk cabbage covered the forest floor. Often she found a few precious cardinal flowers to fill Grandmother's earthen vase.

Glancing toward the freshly worked ground near the cabin, Susanna noticed a few stumps remaining in the area where Grandfather had permitted the Ulrich orphans to plant Indian corn. Into each hill they had placed a fish and then dropped the seed.

While they had planted corn, they talked about Ulrich matters. Catherine had explained how Grandfather was related to them. ". . . And Peter is named after our father. Christopher is named after our grandfather. I am named after our mother."

It feels good to belong somewhere, Susanna decided as she entered the cabin.

"You stacked enough wood for a blizzard, and tomorrow is May," Peter interrupted Susanna's dreaming.

"Even in hot July it takes wood to cook for you hungry boys," she reminded him.

Susanna grinned and went to help Grandmother. She sniffed the smell of turkey pot pie. Peter had killed the turkey in the forest yesterday. "Mmm! The supper smells good, Grandma. You cook the best meals in the Conestoga Valley!" Susanna praised her.

Familiar with Peter's words, Fluff Ball bounded away from him.

For a moment their eyes met. "Susanna, you've been a good helper today, and you speak kindly," Grandmother spoke tenderly. "I'm thankful for a 'granddaughter' like you."

Her words made Susanna feel good. Susanna loved Margaret Huber who had cared for her as long as she could remember.

Then Aunt Anna followed Catherine in the door with milk, butter, and schnitz (dried apple) pies for supper. Aunt Anna, who was older than Catherine, had returned home after working away for awhile. She was like another big sister to Catherine and Susanna.

An impatient white ball of wool squeezed between Anna and the doorway and tried to snatch a schnitz pie. Aunt Anna tried to push the lamb's nose away, but it was useless.

Christopher scolded the naughty lamb. "No, Fluff Ball; schnitz pies are for us. Here, follow me." He grabbed a piece of bread, and Fluff Ball's feet clickety clicked on the clay floor after him. Her legs looked like four sticks of black wood.

Those stick legs make her look special, Susanna thought fondly of the pet that had followed them since she was born.

Around the table Christopher ran with Fluff Ball at his heels. This was Fluff Ball's usual way to get her supper, and it was one of those happy moments in the Huber cabin.

"Time to sleep now; we are hungry, too," Christopher shouted after four rounds. Familiar with Christopher's words, Fluff Ball bounded away from him, but Christopher caught her, shoved her into her box, and barred the door.

"There! We can't leave you outside for the panthers and wolves to eat," he explained to the disappointed lamb. She bleated sadly and then chewed loudly on her hard crust. Then she nestled down into the straw for the night.

The ministers smiled at the bit of pleasure which was not to be avoided even when company arrived.

Unexpectedly, the wind blew the upper part of the cabin door closed with a bang. Rain pelted on the wood-shingled roof. "This will make the crops grow!" Grandfather exclaimed. He and the visitors rejoiced with his brought-together-family around the long oak table. Hans and Margaret purposed that their home would be filled with love, and it was.

After supper, Grandfather directed, "Let us kneel down and pray." The Hubers, Ulrichs, Benedict Brackbill, and Hans Herr knelt as Brother Herr asked God for forgiveness, for protection through the night, and for grace to face tomorrow.

As Susanna crawled into her straw tick, she thought, happily, *Tomorrow, maybe, someone will tell us what our ministers talked about, and we shall find out who this special lady is.*

"As a tick chases away the noise, so also the lovely things about us help children to forget big people's problems," Grandmother told Susanna. Then she whispered, "Goodnight," and bade Susanna to go to sleep.

The patter of rain, the whistling wind, and the sound of voices downstairs drifted farther away.

In my cozy tick is a lovely place to be, was Susanna's last sweet thought.

Chapter 5

Thief

Jacob Huber's daughter, Maria, who was Susanna's age, waited with Susanna, Peter, and Christopher outside Grandfather's cabin. The four of them and Catherine had planned to walk with Grandfather and Grandmother to the Sunday meeting at Grafs.

"Our Indian corn is up," Susanna pointed toward the rows of hills. "I hope the crows don't bother it." She felt an urgent tugging at her skirt and a nose rubbing her fingers.

"Fluff Ball," Peter scolded, "you can't go with us to the meeting." He dragged her into Grandmother's sheep pen. "There, now you'll be safe," he assured the unhappy lamb.

"In Germantown they give bounty for fox and wolf scalps," Christopher informed them. "A bounty would help the wild animal population here, too."

"I wish they'd give a bounty for squirrel tails. Those charming creatures steal every nut and ear of corn that we gather," Maria complained.

Maria was always ready to say what she thought, but Susanna was quiet. In spite of their difference, they still were the best of friends.

"I'd have a dozen pigs thriving on acorns if the bears wouldn't like pork," Peter added. He had been disappointed when during the night a mother bear and her cubs had made a feast of his two-week-old pigs.

They followed Grandfather to the Horseshoe Trail and then chose the short path to the Grafs. The trail wound in and around the largest of oak trees. A high roof of unbroken foliage choked out the brush and encouraged the grass to grow. As they walked on the soft padded floor in the coolness and shade, they were refreshed. Gradually, the light ahead brought into view the plush meadow surrounding the springs. The waters from the three gurgling springs joined to make one stream of the best-tasting water that Susanna knew.

Eight years earlier, Hans Graf's oldest son, Jacob, and their hired man were looking for runaway horses. When they found these trees, they knew that the soil was the best and that the springs never went dry. When Hans saw it, he was pleased and determined that he and his family would make their home in this elysian dale.

Grandfather led them beside the run which nestled snugly between the high forest walls. As the path made a slight turn, a three-sided structure under a spreading oak tree came into view. Morning sunlight spread under the partly-lifted bear hide onto the two log walls behind.

"That place is too small to shelter a family with children," Aunt Anna remarked. "Didn't Hans Graf's wife complain of the cold the winter they stayed here?"

"Not in my hearing," Grandmother assured her. "Anna was grateful that Hans so graciously supplied her a shelter. But she was eager to see the roof on their cabin where they live now. She split the shingles and hung them herself in the moonlight. They needed to dry in the cool as long as possible to keep their edges from curling. At the first meeting in their home she said, 'Welcome to our home in this elysian dale!'"

Only the gobbles of a flock of turkeys and the singing of birds were heard in the forest's stillness. Susanna enjoyed these quiet Sunday morning walks with Grandfather. *Maybe now is a good time to ask Grandfather what the preachers came for*, she decided.

Suddenly, Catherine's voice broke the silence. "Beissel is as sly as a fox, Grandfather. Can't something be done to keep him from stealing our Mennonite people?"

I've never seen her so upset, Susanna thought, as she noticed Catherine's troubled face.

"Hans Graf says that Beissel will never be happy until he has stolen members from every religious group in Penn's Woods," Peter explained. "Why doesn't he preach to the Indians?"

"Do you think the 3,000 Indians scattered about us can trust him?" Grandfather asked.

"Hardly," Peter replied.

Susanna found a tiny white Indian pipe to show to Grandfather once they stopped talking. Grandfather saw it and prodded Peter further. "So Hans thinks Beissel is like this mushroom that lives on rotted wood. The only way he can exist is to live off others."

Hans Graf's "Jacob's staff," the dark tool leaning against the wall, was the surveying tool that Hans Graf used. It was purchased by Frank Stauffer at Levi Groff's sale. It is thought that one of Hans's sons had it since it was listed in Hans's inventory. The swamp spade on the left was used to cut and clean meadow irrigation ditches. This was owned by Marks Groff II, whose will mentions a south race and a north race on Graf's Run, south of Farmersville in Lancaster County, Pa. (Lancaster Mennonite Historical Society, Lancaster, Pa.)

"Right!" Peter replied. "At the mill the other day someone asked Beissel what he believes. He invited them to his meetings to find out."

"What's wrong with that?" Grandfather challenged Peter. "We invite people to our meetings, too."

"Shouldn't we chase those away who work on Sunday?" Catherine wondered.

"Beissel worships on Saturday and works on Sunday. His members are afraid that he will make them do as he does."

"If we chase him away, we'd be like the religious groups who chased us out of Europe," Grandfather answered. "Do you want a church-and-state government like they had in Europe? Do you want a Mennonite government? William Penn wants freedom of religion in Penn's Woods. We may be sent away if we rise up against others' beliefs."

"But how do we protect ourselves from people like Beissel?" Catherine asked thoughtfully. "Beissel says that Hans Graf can't provide for two wives as our bishops have told him to do. He suggested that Hans live in solitude, like himself, and allow someone else to care for his family."

Susanna and Maria looked at each other wide-eyed. *Hans Graf has two wives! So that's why the ministers came last night*, they thought.

"Is it right for Hans to live with Anna if he has another wife?" Peter wanted to know.

"Children, didn't you wonder why Hans recently returned to his earlier work of trading?" Grandfather asked. "Didn't it seem strange to you that we never saw Hans at home except when we have church?"

"Yes, it seemed strange that lately he and Peter spent more of their time trading than farming," Catherine replied. "It seemed that Hans should be home with his children. Once I heard that he slept at the home of his brother Martin, and I wondered why. I never imagined that there might be a reason."

"This explains some things," Peter exclaimed. "I have been wondering how Hans can survey the future road between here and Philadelphia while he is also working at the mill stone he wants to use at the new mill he plans to build. He never seems to be at home, what with doing all these time-consuming things he plans to do at other places.

"Hans and his wives are willing to go beyond what the bishops require of them," Grandfather added.

"Who is Hans's other wife?" Christopher asked. "How did he get two wives?"

Grandfather proceeded to tell how it happened, as the group continued their Sunday walk.

"Hans's father was a rich and important government man in Switzerland. He wanted Hans to be an army general. Hans trained

Peter Graf's mill located along Graf's Run near the Groffdale Lancaster Conference Church. The building may have been styled somewhat after the mill that his father, Hans Graf, had built earlier. The limestone rocks are beautiful.

for that and then married Magdelena, his first wife. After their marriage, Hans became an Anabaptist. Willingly, he left his riches and promising future behind and was baptized. Because of past contacts with merchant seamen in Holland, he wanted to help our brethren come to America.

"But Magdelena didn't share his Anabaptist beliefs. She did not wish to leave the state church, so Hans left Switzerland without her. Almost thirty years ago he arrived in Philadelphia with some of our brethren. A number of times he returned secretly to Magdelena and pled with her to come to America. The law stated that if his parents or wife helped him in any way, they would be fined and imprisoned. Not wishing to hurt them, Hans soon left Switzerland.

"When their son, Jacob, was five years old, Hans brought him to Germantown. Soon afterward, some immigrants informed Hans that Magdelena had died. After a time Hans married Anna Herr, Martin Kendig's niece. Hans and Anna moved to Strasburg and soon had several children.

"Eight years ago, Hans's brother, Martin Graf, arrived in Philadelphia. He was baffled at Hans's marriage, because Magdelena was still living! After a time, Martin took courage and asked Hans how he could rightfully have two living wives. Hans was shocked and perplexed! He had not known that Magdelena was alive. The report of his wife's death was false; another lady by the same name had died. What should he do?

"Jacob, when he was older and had a family, wanted to help his mother come to Graf's Run. It was then that Martin Kendig volunteered to make the dangerous trip and find her. Soon after his arrival in Holland, he met Magdelena. She was an Anabaptist and was coming to America to find Hans. It was hard for her to believe what had happened, but she took the blame. Hans's letter and money to pay her ship fare convinced her to come. God had led the way.

"Eight years after they discovered that Magdelena was living, Hans and Jacob saw their wife and mother in Germantown. Today we will welcome her at our meeting. She is living with Jacob and his family until Hans builds a cabin and barn for her," Grandfather concluded.

"Why does Beissel think that Hans can't provide for two wives?" Catherine asked again. "Next thing, Beissel will steal Hans Graf, too."

"He thinks that such an arrangement would cause jealousy and ill feelings. But, when three people determine to do right, God will make a way for them to do it," Grandfather assured her. "Beissel's idea of how Hans should live is not correct. The Scripture says, 'But if any provide not for his own . . . he . . . is worse than an infidel' (I Timothy 5:8)."

"Hans doesn't need to live in solitude to live right. The Scriptures and our leaders tell Hans what to do," Grandfather explained. "His boys are old enough to help Jacob with the farming. This way Hans can be away from home serving others and still care for his family. Hans is a respected, faithful witness everywhere he goes."

"How can we keep Beissel from stealing our people?" Catherine asked Grandfather again.

"We are all wondering the same thing," Grandfather said sympathetically. "How can we keep every strange doctrine from overtaking us? Brother Benedict will minister to us this morning on what the Scriptures say concerning this. You children listen carefully. There is a way."

I hope that Beissel doesn't steal any more of us, Susanna mused, as her family continued on their way to the meeting.

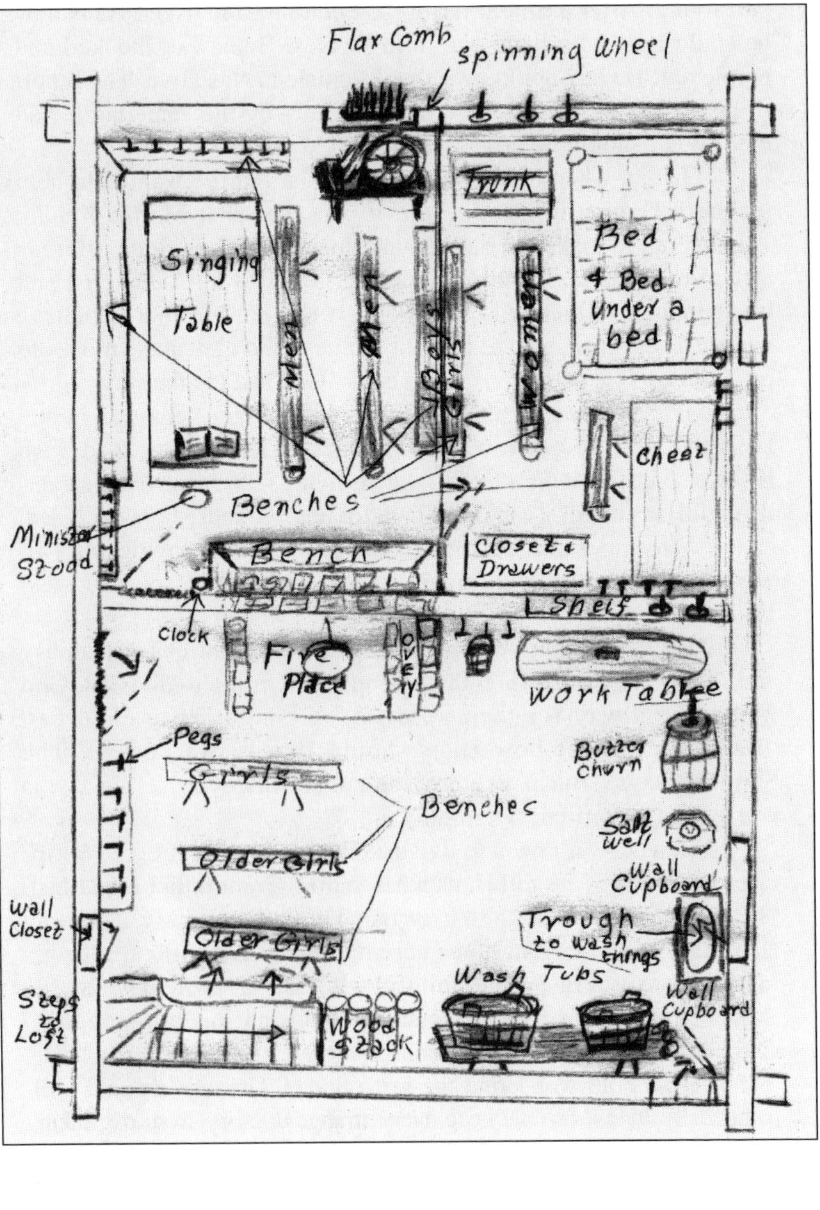
Flax Comb
Spinning Wheel
Trunk
Bed
+ Bed
Under a
bed
Singing
Table
Men
Men
Boys
Girls
Women
Chest
Benches
Minister
Stood
Bench
Closet &
Drawers
Shelf
Clock
Fire
Place
Oven
Work Table
Pegs
Girls
Benches
Butter
churn
Salt
well
Older Girls
Wall
Cupboard
Trough
to wash
things
Older Girls
Wall
Closet
Wash Tubs
Wall
Cupboard
Steps
to
Loft
Wood
Stack

CHAPTER 6

Make The Grike Narrow

As her family neared Grafs' cabin, Susanna saw Quick Foot and his family ahead of them. Quick Foot and his wife had become Mennonites.

"Let's catch up to Bright Star, and then find Feronica," Maria suggested to Susanna. Feronica Graf, who was Hans Graf's daughter, and Bright Star, who was Quick Foot's daughter, were both ten like Susanna and Maria.

"Father's first wife is here today!" Feronica greeted them in excitement. "Yesterday I helped her plant saffron bulbs, rosemary, and other herbs."

"Is the cabin which they built for her close to the lookout?" Bright Star asked. Her black eyes sparkled with curiosity.

"It is on the cliff below the lookout," Feronica informed them. "My brothers are building a stone wall around her place. They made four grikes so she can easily slip through the wall."

"I hope the grike is wide enough for Magdelena to pull her skirts through," Maria commented.

"Yes, grikes are a fat man's agony, but Magdelena is a thin lady. She will glide through gracefully," Feronica laughed. "Mother says that we will help her to plant her garden tomorrow. I can hardly wait."

"You'd better go in. Jacob is at the singing table," Catherine reminded the girls. They followed her to the big girls' bench in the kitchen. From there they filed past the long table for the singers in the next room. Peter, Christopher, and the Graf boys were already seated on a bench against the wall behind the table.

In the next room the girls sat down on their bench which faced the women's bench against the opposite wall. Between them was a bed. A pleasant-looking lady sat between Anna Graf and Grandmother.

That is Magdelena Graf, Susanna knew. She saw tears in Magdelena's eyes and hoped that she felt welcome.

Ausbund *used by Hans Graf with his son's name—Samuel Graff—in large letters. The printing at the top reads in German: "This book belongs to me, Hans Graff. It has cost 6 shillings."*
(Muddy Creek Farm Library)

    Susanna did not realize how grateful Magdelena was to be here. Magdelena had suffered much, but rather than pitying herself, she had given herself to help others. When Magdelena smiled at her, Susanna knew nothing of Magdelena's thoughts. Magdelena determined to help this young orphan girl as she would face the difficulties of frontier life.

    Sister Nagele and Johannes Landis's wife and children were missing. Brother Nagele would not be coming in with the ministers either. Their places were empty. Feronica told Susanna that they had been baptized another time—and under the water at that. Grandfather's persecutors in Europe had considered it wicked for adults to be baptized even once.

    Silently, Susanna counted how many people were in the Graf cabin. There were eleven of Hans Graf's family—they had six boys and three girls. Jacob Graf's family totaled five. There were five in the family of Hans's brother, Martin Graf. (The Ebys had gone to the Strasburg meeting.) There were three in Quick Foot's family;

seven in Jacob Huber's; and seven in Grandfather's, counting the four Ulrichs, which made thirty-eight in all. Beissel had stolen eight, including the minister.

On the Sundays when they met at the Ebys' on Mill Creek, many neighbors came also. There was much commotion at the Mill Creek meetings because the Eicher girls and the Hildebrand girl wanted to go into solitude like Beissel.

Susanna knew every word of the songs that Jacob led from his song book, the *Ausbund*. There were only enough books for those at the singers' table, so they sang the same songs many times. The songs expressed the deep feelings of the older people who had suffered much in persecution. Susanna hoped that terrible times would never come to Penn's Woods.

After the second song, the ministers came in and sat down at the singers' table. Next, Deacon Martin Graf read from the Bible and announced that Brother Benedict would preach. Susanna could not see Brother Benedict because of the wall, but his voice rang with conviction and immediately caught everyone's attention.

He read from Acts, chapter fifteen, and spoke of the need for protection from false doctrine. "The church in that day had problems, too. They made safeguards to keep themselves pure. We make pens and fences to protect our lambs. We need fences for ourselves, also," he emphasized.

"Persecution was our fence in Europe," he reminded them. "It was crude and ugly like a root fence, but it held us together.

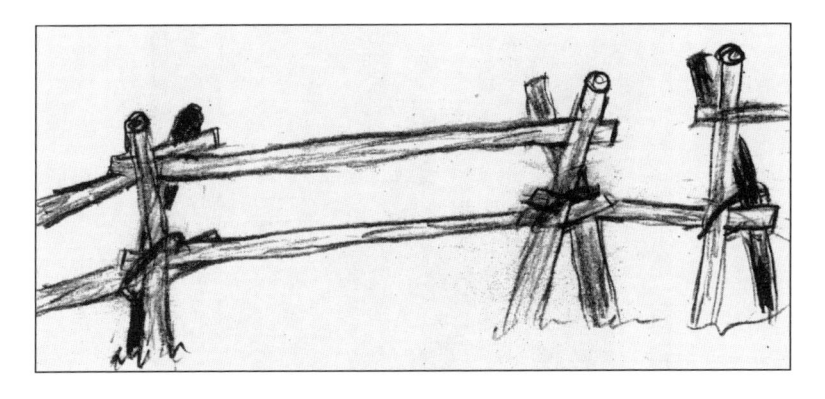

A stake and rider fence with a grike (break in the top of the fence that girls with skirts could step over).

Here we have no persecution, so we need another kind of fence. A stone wall or stake and rider fence are like a scriptural discipline. Build the grike narrow enough to keep our lambs at home and the foxes outside. Submit to the Scriptures rather than ideas of men. Refrain from attending Beissel's meetings," he pled. "We have lost enough today."

Later, Brother Herr announced that there would be no more meetings at Mill Creek because of the disturbance they made.

Susanna listened closely to all that was said. Their ministers wanted to keep them safe. She was not sure how they would make a narrow grike, but she felt good as Brother Benedict offered his solemn benedictory prayer.

An old broad axe. (*Mifflin County Mennonite Historical Society*)

24

CHAPTER 7

Linsey-Woolsey

"It's winter!" Susanna cried with excitement as she peered out the cabin door. The Saeue Schwamm forest trees were drooping with snow, the whiteness glistening in the morning sun.

Susanna closed the door and whispered, "Grandmother, Quick Foot is coming with Grandfather."

Grandmother looked interested. A happy smile appeared on her face. "Keep knitting your stocking, Susanna, and we shall soon hear what he has to say," Grandmother bade her. Grandmother stopped her spinning wheel and began gathering things for Quick Foot to take home with him. When she added a linsey-woolsey baby gown and blanket to the pile, Susanna became curious.

Susanna's needles kept clicking as she listened and watched. As long as she could remember, she knew that to get new stockings, you must knit them yourself. Susanna could hear the chopping of Jacob's broadaxe as he squared beams for the addition to their cabin. The moment was filled with expectancy.

Quick Foot unlaced the rawhide cords of his wooden snowshoes and propped them against the wall. He removed his fur cap and buckskin robe and joined Grandfather in front of the fire. The puddles around his buckskin leggings grew larger and larger.

He must have something important to say after walking so far through this deep snow, Susanna was sure.

After a time, Grandmother could hold her question no longer. "Will you be needing this yet?" she inquired, as she held the linsey-woolsey gown in front of Quick Foot.

He grinned broadly. "Yes, my dear wife needs this. It is a boy. His name is Seeking Hart. As the hart panteth after the water brooks, so we pray that our son might seek for truth."

Susanna's thoughts jumped with delight. *Bright Star has a baby brother!* She remembered when she and Bright Star played

25

Indian games. Bright Star could run like a deer. She always won. Now she would have a brother to play with.

Later, when Susanna thought he might be leaving, Quick Foot spoke again. "Linsey-woolsey reminds me of something else that I've come to talk about."

How can linsey-woolsey be like anything else? Susanna asked herself.

The cabin was quiet except for the clicking of needles. "Linsey-woolsey is a soft material woven from a mixture of wool and flax," Quick Foot reminded Grandfather. "But, there are mixtures of other things around here that aren't so desirable."

"There are mixtures," Grandfather agreed. "Which ones are bothering you?"

"There is such a mixture of ideas in Beissel's group," Quick Foot began. "At first his followers loved him and clung to him. They were impressed with his spirited preaching. Now many are suspicious of him because he preaches strange ideas. His followers shake their heads sadly and declare that he is out of his mind."

"I saw him preach with his eyes closed," Quick Foot spoke excitedly. "He claimed that wonderful mysteries of heaven were revealed to him. The things which he saw seemed strange to me. Some people left the meeting. Suddenly, Beissel cried, 'The mysteries are again sealed. The spirit retires in his secret chamber.' Those who remained quarreled with Beissel the rest of the night."

"I'm glad our brethren submit to each other's ideas," Grandfather returned with a sigh of relief.

"Now they are building little cabins on Nagele's place," Quick Foot went on. "Nagele is sending poor immigrants from Germantown to settle here. Who is going to feed all of these people?"

Cabins on Nagele's place! I'd like to see them, Susanna wished silently.

"If Nagele doesn't feed them, we will," Grandfather assured Quick Foot. "My wife has filled the loft, the haymow, the ground cellar, the smokehouse, and the springhouse with all kinds of food. There was plenty of grain this year. The poorest man can eat rabbit, squirrel, deer, and twenty-pound turkeys from the forest."

Susanna could see part of the loft's intriguing array above them. Strings laden with beans amidst bags of dried apples, pears, and grapes hung from the ceiling. Behind them, baskets of wheat, corn, oats, and buckwheat lined the walls. They stopped the cold wind that crept through the cracks between the logs. Paths around the groups of nuts and teas on the floor made walking exciting. A grass-woven tray of sliced fruit hung from the ceiling in front of the chimney, with rows of fruit continually drying on that tray. The tangy aroma was a constant reminder that there was an abundance of food.

Under the hay in the barn, squash, pumpkin, and cabbage stayed fresh and did not freeze. Cheese, salted-down butter and meat and crocks of apple and pear butter were kept cold in the springhouse. Rows of cured shoulders, hams, bacons, and venison hung in the smokehouse.

In the ground cellar were turnips, beets, apples, and pears. Most fascinating was the small pile of round tubers in the corner which Quick Foot had given them to plant in the garden. Next spring they would sprout and each sprout would produce a big stalk of many more tubers, which the English called potatoes. A baked potato covered with brown butter was a treat for Susanna. The smell of food was everywhere. She wiggled her nose with satisfaction.

"Since the food shortage three years ago, we have learned to preserve food," she heard Grandfather say. "Nagele's poor people are coming; Martin Kendig is bringing more Mennonites from Europe; and we must feed them all."

There was a long silence.

"But what is your problem, Quick Foot?" Grandfather urged him to talk further.

"Nagele's cows have eaten our corn," Quick Foot admitted reluctantly. "Last night they feasted greedily at our corn cratch."

"A cratch is made to keep corn out of an animal's reach. How could the cows get to the corn?" Grandfather wondered.

"When they pushed the cratch over, the boards broke and the corn rolled on the ground," Quick Foot explained. "Many Indians have no food for the winter because the white men's cows stray around their wigwams."

"We'll share our food with you—all that you need," Grandfather consoled him. "Our brethren will share with other needy Indians whom you

Cratch

know. We'll do all we can to help our white men build fences. Jacob and I will help Nagele to repair the fence around his pasture unless he wishes to do it himself."

"Nagele won't repair his fence," Quick Foot lamented. "He is busy preaching Beissel's doctrines down east."

"Then I'll ask some of those poor people in his cabins to help," Grandfather insisted.

"They are too busy meditating on Beissel's heavenly manna. I'll help you," Quick Foot offered.

"Agreed!" Grandfather sounded pleased. "We'll build the fence strong. Let's chase the cows in his barn this evening. I'll feed them until the snow melts. Then we'll ask the Graf boys to help us repair his fence."

"You are returning good for evil. But what if they claim your child at their next meeting?" Quick Foot warned Grandfather. "You were here before them. Hans Graf shared his land with Nagele. Now Nagele steals your people from your faith. Why don't you make them leave?"

"What would Governor Keith think of us German aliens fighting over land which neither of us own?" Grandfather questioned Quick Foot. "After fourteen years the English are allowing us to become citizens. But first we'll have to say how much we are worth and state our peculiar religious views."

"Governor Keith would send all of you back to Switzerland," Quick Foot declared with certainty. "If you can fight each other, you can fight for Keith, also."

Susanna recalled the awful stories of her people's persecutions and the loss of lives on the sea. *Never do we wish to go back to Europe*, she cried within.

"Indians and Mennonites are chased from one place to another," Quick Foot talked on. "Mennonites and some Indians stay on English land, but the English fear us. Now the English accept German Mennonites as citizens, but we are not welcome here."

Grandfather looked at Quick Foot closely and then spoke carefully. "You are the first red man to tell me how you feel. Never will I take from you that right to be equal. William Penn has given us the first freedom in this world's history. He welcomes the red man to this place, too. It is the greed of wicked men which wrongs you."

"Never fear, there will always be a place for you among our brethren. We can always rejoice that we are all citizens of heaven."

"How do we help our Seeking Harts to choose right, with Beissel nearby waiting to teach them wrong?" Quick Foot asked.

"By making peace. We need to teach truth and respect our leaders' fences. Strong fences keep stray cattle and doctrines where they belong," Grandfather chuckled. He picked up an ash spoke for a wheel and began carving.

"You are making a wagon," Quick Foot noted.

"Yes, and it takes all kinds of wood to make a good wagon," Grandfather replied. "The best wagon is not heavy. It will not wear away or break easily. Wood must work beside wood in both dry and damp weather. We use oak for the framework, elm for the side and floor. The spokes and shafts must be ash, and the slats must be hickory. Finally, the seat must be pine.

"It's not the mixture of races, nationalities, and religions that matters, but how well we can respect each other. Only the peace of God in our hearts can give us dignity and wisdom to do this. Only then will the Conestoga Valley be a linsey-woolsey place to live."

Quick Foot lifted the bag of food over his shoulder. The linsey-woolsey baby things were carefully wrapped and tied on the top of the bag. His broad grin and quick bow to the ladies said his thank you. "I must go home to my dear wife with all these good things and thoughts. When you come to chase the cows home, I will be ready," he assured Grandfather.

"Thank you, thank you," he called, after his snowshoes were fastened.

CHAPTER 8

Freedom At Last

Susanna stooped to pick up another piece of firewood. She listened. From the west echoed sounds of someone chopping wood.

"Grandmother," she shouted as she dashed into the cabin, "those Eckerlins from Germantown must have bought Johannes Hildebrand's old cabin! Someone is chopping wood over there."

"Quickly, run to the barn and tell Grandfather," Grandmother instructed her.

In spite of Susanna's eleven-year-old clumsiness, she bounded over the frozen path, unmindful of the icy wind that stung her face.

When Grandfather heard the news, he became alive with joy. "Tell Grandmother to get ready and we will walk over," Grandfather directed. "What a cool reception Conestoga Valley's March winds have given them today. And hurry," he added.

Susanna ran back to the cabin. *At times like this, Grandfather and Grandmother treat us Ulrichs like their children,* she thought, feeling very much included.

Soon they were following the footpath through the forest to their new neighbors. Christopher pulled a sled loaded with provisions for them.

As they neared the cabin, Susanna saw two young men. One was chopping wood; the other one was carrying an armful of wood through the cabin door which was opened by Magdelena Graf. *These must be the Eckerlins,* Susanna decided. *Grandfather and Grandmother were friends with them in Europe. Their father was a pietist preacher.*

Magdelena's presence meant that someone was sick. So soon she had become Conestoga Valley's nurse. Grandmother noticed her and said, "Someone must be ill. Traveling the Minquas Path was probably worse than they expected."

Someday Susanna wished to travel on the Minquas Path, which was the most direct route from Philadelphia to Harris Ferry. Every traveler on that trail had an exciting story.

"Likely they came quickly because of the warm spell these last four days," Grandfather figured aloud.

"Are you Michael Eckerlin's boys?" Grandfather's friendly words attracted the youth who had stopped chopping to welcome them.

"Did you know our father?" the older boy asked, with a look of surprise. "My name is Israel, and this is my younger brother, Gabriel."

"Yes, I knew your father well. When your older brother, Samuel, was young, he carried many pieces of wood for me," Grandfather informed them.

Gabriel gave them a friendly smile, and immediately Susanna liked him. Israel acted aloof toward Grandfather.

Catherine and Susanna followed Grandmother in the door at Magdelena's bidding.

"Do you have a weary traveler here?" Grandmother asked.

"Yes. The Eckerlins and Christopher and Marie Sauer and their son arrived with Hans Graf last night," Magdelena told them. "The Eckerlin boys started a fire, and Hans sent for Feronica and me. Mother Eckerlin was very cold and exhausted on arrival. We all know about the four-day tramp up the Minquas Path, followed with springtime's bottomless mud on Peters Road."

"Yes, indeed, we all know about that," Grandmother repeated with mutual understanding.

Susanna and Catherine joined Feronica Graf beside the kettle of steaming broth and vegetables. On a nearby bed, a woman peered expectantly at Grandmother from under her tick.

"Margaret Koch Huber!" she exclaimed.

"Anna Henderson Eckerlin!" Grandmother returned, and they greeted each other as old-time friends. The girls watched as the two ladies wept tears of bliss.

"Unbelievable! After thirty-six years of our horrible past, God has permitted us to meet again," Grandmother cried.

"Our grandparents remembered our people being imprisoned and martyred from their childhood," Anna reminded them. "Our parents remembered when they fled their homes in Switzerland. They hid in the forest as they traveled many days to the Palatinate. There, along the Rhine River we played, always fearful of that day the papal hierarchy might send us away. We Anabaptists believed in separation of church and state; they didn't. Our time to live under their government was limited."

Anna's voice shook because of the awful memories, so Grandmother continued. "And that moment came in 1689. It was an extremely cold winter. Snow covered the fields and vineyards, which already lay in waste from previous wars. Louis XIV sent his generals, Montclas and Melac, to end our existence forever.

"The dwellings of half a million people were burned. After the fires had ceased, we were exposed to the merciless weather and cruel starvation. This heartless destruction meant one thing: if you desire religious freedom, go elsewhere."

"Is it any wonder every mean dog in Europe and Philadelphia is called Melac?" Magdelena interrupted.

"Where could we go? Our hearts bled with sorrow beyond any words which we could express," Grandmother continued her story. "A faint hope of America, that faraway land, flickered in the back of our minds. In one year's time, 30,000 of us moved down the Rhine River toward Holland. Would God help us to go to that peaceful home in Penn's Woods? All that we possessed hung on our backs. We had no idea of how we would pay our ship fare, so we prayed that God would provide.

"After weeks of walking in the cold and sleeping on any pile of straw in sight, we arrived in Holland. There were so many of us, yet the Holland Mennonites fed and clothed us all. The world knew of our plight and showed mercy in many ways. In 1708, Queen Anne invited us to England. We sailed northward on a fleet of ships and hoped for something better.

"On arrival, they placed us in camps and fed us. There were so many of us that apparently they were not prepared. Food became scarce, and medical assistance was hard to find. When a flu epidemic arrived, 10,000 of our group died. There was such discouragement that 7,000 returned to Germany, hopeful for an easier way of survival.

"On December 25 of the next year, 4,000 of us were packed on ten ships and sent to America. In the living quarters there was only a two-by-six-foot space per person. We knew that was too close for many to survive the trip through those cold winter months. Would God, in His mercy, spare any of us? For three months huge blocks of ice accompanied us on the dark waters. It seemed that only God's mercy kept them from dashing the ship to pieces. When warmer days arrived, food became scarce. We were weak and hungry and almost gave up hope of ever seeing land again. Only half of us who left London remained, but we kept praying.

"When we heard that land was in sight, it hardly seemed true. We cried and thanked God as we sailed up the Hudson River. Never again did we wish to hear the roar of ocean waters.

"Finally, we set foot on an island further up the river. That summer we lived in tents. Our seventy orphans clung to us until, one by one, they were apprenticed to the English.

"Then Peter Ulrichs, along with others, were sent up the Hudson River to manufacture tar. In time, this would repay the charges of their transportation and substance. Governor Hunter used violent measures to make them work hard. Peter and his wife both became weakened, which was the cause of their deaths in later years. Their first child, Catherine, was born there.

"Hans and I and our children settled in the Schoharie Valley with others who had come with us. We cleared the land as we were told to do, but soon we learned that our suspicions were true. Our land titles were defective. Again, we asked God to make a way to Penn's Woods. William Penn heard of our plight and provided us with a wagon. With much rejoicing, we, along with Peter Ulrich's family, traveled south to Germantown. Peter's little boys, Peter and Christopher, came with us. Within a year, Susanna, their fourth child, was born. Soon after that, both parents died, leaving four orphans in our care. In the spring of 1717, we traveled on the Minquas Path with Hans Graf to the Conestoga Valley."

There was silence after Grandmother finished. Susanna took a deep breath and wiped her tears. Never before had she heard so much of the story at once.

Anna Eckerlin sat up in bed and began talking again. "My husband was responsible for a group of Anabaptists not far from the Holland border, so we stayed there. On arrival in Germantown last year, we learned to know Nagele, your runaway preacher. He urged us to attend his meetings, but we didn't go. The Mennonites discouraged us from becoming involved with Beissel. We all know how Beissel's doctrines have been tried in Germany. Their groups became immoral and disintegrated."

"Beissel gets around. He has quite a few groups in Penn's Woods calling for him," Margaret commented.

"One of Nagele's co-workers often visited our home," Anna continued. "He explained his idea of proper Christian living. I am a Mennonite, but I fear he has influenced my boys wrongly. My sons know nothing of temptations of people who live in solitude. At first it appears attractive. The only safe way is to heed the advice of older persons who understand such things.

"On the ocean Israel vowed that he would serve God if he ever reached land, but he seems to have forgotten that promise. He was very gullible when it came to the easy-to-get mammon in Germantown. We were advised to come here where everyone lives in great simplicity. Can you direct us to your meeting place tomorrow?"

"Certainly. I'll stay until tomorrow and walk with you to our meeting at Grafs," Magdelena offered. "By then you should be on your feet."

"I'm getting on my feet now," Anna groaned with determination as her stiff legs and feet moved into action. Magdelena and Grandmother helped her to stand.

Susanna winced as she watched Anna slowly move. The women wrapped Anna in a sheepskin and handed her a bowl of broth. *Where is Anna's husband and her son, Samuel?* Susanna wondered.

"This pain is nothing in comparison to the sufferings of the past. It is like heaven to have freedom at last," Anna cried with joy. Her listeners understood.

Chapter 9

Springless Wagon

"Hello," Hans Huber greeted the women inside the cabin.

Grandfather and the four boys stood at the door watching. The Eckerlins wore buckskin trousers like the Conestoga Valley Mennonites. Their shirts were made of the same brown cloth which Mennonites used for dresses and shirts.

"Where is your husband and Samuel?" Grandfather ventured to ask after they shook hands. "I remember Michael's fiery preaching and his firm beliefs in simplicity. He considered the rich man's carriage a vanity. On his circuits to meetings he chose to walk rather than ride."

Anna's eyes filled with tears as she began to share her deepest hurt. "In 1705, when Samuel was two and our daughter was a baby, Michael was expelled from the Alsace. He had refused to stop the pietist gatherings in our home. We fled various places among kinsmen and finally arrived in Schwarzenau. There we joined the German Baptist movement. Mennonite Anabaptists had been welcomed there because of their development of the textile industry. The German Baptists' beliefs were so similar to the Mennonites that they were accepted also. We learned to appreciate the Mennonites who lived around us.

"Magdalena, that's where we met your husband and your son, Jacob. Hans had been to Penn's Woods at least twice before and had returned to urge you to go there with him. Soon they left for America, taking Anabaptists with them. Hans knew the seamen and the perils of the sea and was able to help others flee for freedom.

"There in Schwarzenau we lived beside you, Hans and Margaret. You cut wood for us when Michael went away for meetings, but so soon you were leaving for England. We and our two little ones said our good-byes to you and your little Jacob when you and Peter Ulrich's family left with you.

"After you left, we moved to Krefeld where our three boys—Emanuel, Israel, and Gabriel—were born. There my husband and

Alexander Mack, who began the German Baptist movement, became close friends. They thought alike in most areas. At that time there was so much false doctrine, it was almost impossible for two Baptist families to even worship together.

"Four years ago when Samuel was nineteen, Michael went with Alexander Mack to visit our brethren who were imprisoned in the fortress of Julich. Visitors were permitted, but my husband was never allowed to return home. Soon after that, he died in prison.

"That left me and the children free to come to come to America. We would have come before if Michael had not been responsible for the group at Krefeld. I sold the caps, which he made in his spare time, to pay our way to America. Our daughter died on the sea, but the rest of us fared well. Samuel and Emanuel will remain in Germantown until Samuel finishes his apprenticeship."

"I am sorry to hear this," Grandmother sympathized. "My German Baptist family thought well of your husband."

"For four days I tried to decide whether to walk or ride in that jolting wagon," Anna changed the subject. "I almost wished for one of those fancy wagons in Germantown. They have springs which make riding more comfortable. But Hans Graf's wagon was almost too full of our belongings for me to ride anyway."

"Margaret, are these your girls?" Anna asked as she looked their way.

"No, our daughter, Anna, will come later with Jacob and his family. This is Peter Ulrich's oldest girl, Catherine, and their youngest child, Susanna," Grandmother motioned toward them.

"You girls both look like your Grandmother Veronica, and our Aunt Veronica Eberly," Anna informed them. "We met Veronica Eberly in Germantown. She is a very brave and determined woman. Hans, here is a letter she wrote to you."

As Grandfather took the letter, Susanna became very curious about this Veronica Eberly, the person she resembled. And what was that letter about?

"Veronica's Baby Ulrich would have died on the sea if Marie Sauer hadn't given him medicine," Anna exclaimed. "The Sauers have a medicine book from Halle University. This spring they will plant herbs to sell. Between the Sauers and Magdelena, Conestoga Valley's people should have good health. We unloaded the Sauers at their cabin. It is very unique, the way Mill Creek bisects their land."

36

"Yes, their land is bordered by Hans Graf's land," Grandmother prompted. "Our run empties into Mill Creek not far from their cabin, so we are neighbors. I've wondered what the Sauers think of Beissel."

"Christopher didn't say what he thought of Beissel on the way here," Anna replied. "He did make it clear that Mennonites are too exclusive. The Mennonite way of simplicity and the German Baptist way of worship are desirable. He believes in voting, but some Mennonites don't vote. He doesn't identify himself with any religious group."

"What makes him so critical of everyone?" Grandmother wondered.

"Remember, back in Schwarzenau, Germany, when Christopher and Marie were fourteen years old?" Anna reminded her. "They were well taught in every religious thought, but did they know any adult who was willing to submit to church authority? Everyone knew of Bishop Hans Zug's well-disciplined group, which was hiding near Darmstadt, but they were considered too strict. For years the pietistic Anabaptists in Schwarzenau never had a regular meeting place. The Sauers must learn to submit if they ever will become a part of any group."

"Did Sauer bring Germantown vanities with him?" Grandmother voiced her concern.

"No," Anna stated emphatically. "The Sauers are rich, but Christopher is opposed to displaying one's wealth. They've come here to live a simpler way."

"Boys, come closer to the fire," Anna invited them. "Can these be Peter Ulrich's boys?"

"Yes, this is Peter and Christopher," Grandfather nodded in their direction.

"After much gain and much loss, God has brought us together again," Anna reminded them.

"In a place where we live a simpler life, did I hear you say?" Grandfather said, repeating Anna's words. "We live simpler, but we all keep working to have it nicer. The Scriptures permit us to enjoy the fruits of our labor, you know."

"It takes more than one man's idea of simplicity to have an elysian dale," Grandmother suggested. "Beissel has peculiar ideas about simplicity."

Anna would still be lying on her back if she had been resting on one of Beissel's board beds, Susanna thought, critically.

"Yes, it takes many counselors to keep a group consistent," Grandfather cautioned. "If our leaders say, 'No springs on your wagons,' then we ride without springs. It is better to identify with the poor than the rich."

"As I walked behind the wagon, I wondered how soon our children would have springs on their wagons," Anna admitted.

"What we ask of our people today may not be so important in the next generation," Grandfather reminded them.

Maybe someday I'll ride in a wagon with springs! Susanna smiled at the idea.

To move a stump, the ox jerked his rope hard and with all his strength gave another pull.

CHAPTER 10

Grandmother's Wooden Bowl

Skillfully, Susanna's aunt, Veronica Ulrich Eberly, kneaded the dough in her wooden bowl. This special bowl reminded Veronica of her grandmother, who believed in hard work and doing it right, even in the midst of difficulty. Today was Veronica's baking day.

In her letter to Grandfather, Veronica had asked if he could help them settle in the Conestoga Valley since her husband had not come with her. As Grandfather prepared an Irish settler's abandoned cabin, Susanna had waited in expectancy. Finally in April, Veronica and her five children had arrived.

Now it was May. The ground had heaved and settled so that tree roots were loosened. Grandfather's ox had pulled Jacob, Peter, and Christopher on the farm sled to the Eberlys' home to pull out tree stumps. Stumps were easier to dislodge with the help of an ox, rather than with a spade and mattock alone. Once the ox was tied to the stump, he knew to give a quick jerk and pull. After the men had loosened the dirt and roots around the stump, Peter yelled. Immediately, the ox jerked his rope hard and with all his strength gave another hard pull. Thus, the small stumps would be removed and pushed on the sled to the root fence. The men would farm around the larger stumps.

Gabriel and Israel Eckerlin arrived to help with the digging.

Catherine, Susanna, and Maria had also come to help Veronica for the day.

"Once the stumps are gone, you'll have a big garden," Catherine commented as she watched Veronica knead her bread.

"I'm eager to plant the pumpkin and bean seeds that Quick Foot gave to us," Veronica replied with enthusiasm.

"This wooden bowl is so smooth. How old is it?" Catherine asked.

"Grandmother Ulrich was born in 1655. Her mother gave it

to her. It is at least seventy years old," Veronica figured. "She never lived in an elysian dale, and I probably won't either, but I can bake bread for ourselves and to help feed the poor."

Susanna admired Veronica's willingness to be useful.

"Magdelena is busy helping sick newcomers," Veronica told them. "The flu is making a hardship for many. Magdelena's nursing is well known. She works in spite of her own disappointment. That is better than waiting alone for a revelation on how to solve one's problems."

"Our neighbor, Daniel Eicher, would like to start German Baptist meetings separate from Beissel," Catherine shared the latest. "He hopes to influence those newly arriving settlers before Beissel does."

"We Mennonites can influence them, too," Veronica added. "It is good our Dortrecht Confession is translated into English so that the Irish and Scotch can know what we believe, also. Some Protestants are becoming alarmed at the insincere promises by which people are allowed to join their churches. Our witness has not only a Confession of Faith, but our leaders are seeing the need to require us to live right. I am satisfied to be a Mennonite."

"Have you heard anything from your husband?" Catherine asked Veronica.

"All we know is that when we were on the ship waiting to leave for America, suddenly he said that he must go back for something. He wouldn't say what it was. The others with us begged him to stay, but he left without saying good-bye. We cried and prayed as the ship set sail, and watched in vain for his return. No one has heard from him since. Thank God, the Hubers have helped us."

"Would you girls like to pick up stones in the garden? Throw them on the fence row," Veronica suggested.

"We'll be glad to," Maria replied as she and Susanna bounded for the door.

"I like to pick up stones," Susanna told Maria. "Here we can watch them move the stumps."

"Look at those Eckerlins!" Maria exclaimed. "Grandmother says their name means 'strong as a bear.' I like the way they work."

As they threw stones into their stone boat, Susanna noticed a very narrow slit in the upper part of the stone wall. "That would be a fat man's agony. Let's slide through there when we empty our stone boat," she suggested.

"Sometime let's slip through a grike and take a long trip," Maria proposed dreamily. "That would bring more pleasure than picking up stones and feeding the poor."

"Where would we travel?" Susanna prodded. "I'd like to go to Philadelphia and then Germantown."

"I'd like to go to Hickorytown, Harris Ferry, and west," Maria envisioned aloud. "I want to see the buffalo herds on the prairie that Peter Bezellion talks about. Since Daniel Eicher killed the last buffalo in Saeue Schwamm, the buffalo trail to the water hole has grown up with weeds. Their trail had been wide enough for two wagons to travel side by side. Traders like Peter Bezellion tell great tales about faraway places. I'd like to see them all."

"Veronica is determined to care for her children. Everyone around here works. Maybe we'd better stay home to make bread to feed the poor," Susanna proposed wisely. "Grandmother Ulrich's wooden bowl and today's stump moving should remind us to be better workers."

"Probably so," Maria agreed.

CHAPTER 11

Smooth As A Well-Worn Wheel

Susanna overheard Grandfather and Grandmother talking in the other room.

"Maudlin Kendig's marriage to Henry Weber will be as smooth as a well-worn wheel," Grandfather said.

Susanna thought so, too. The girls said that Henry had laid a board floor in their cabin and bought her one of those new cast iron stoves. Indeed, Maudlin's happy face was admired by every girl at the meeting on Sunday.

She listened as Grandmother spoke. "Maudlin and Henry were both mature enough to marry. They are quite a contrast to Henry's brother and his wife. She married too young. Now she is begging to leave her little ones and go with Beissel. Where does she get ideas to treat her husband like that? He has stopped preaching until she gets settled."

"Jacob and Barbara Graf have a rough marriage, also. One day they are with us and the next day they are with Beissel," Grandfather added sadly.

"I'm not sure about Catherine marrying Samuel Eckerlin," Grandmother had said.

Grandfather said more words in favor of Catherine marrying, and it was at that moment that Susanna had heard enough. They did not realize she was in there. Her eavesdropping must come to an end. *Catherine is marrying Samuel!*

Quietly, Susanna tiptoed out the door and ran. In her haste to get away, she stubbed her toe on a stone. What she had heard was as painful as her throbbing toe.

As she dipped her bleeding toe into the creek, Susanna couldn't imagine what the future would hold without Catherine. The spinning wheel in the corner of Grandmother's cabin would never again make comforting music on rainy days. The joys of chinking and dubbing the cracks in the walls with Catherine would be over.

I should have guessed why Deacon Martin Graf visited with Grandfather and Catherine, Susanna scolded herself. *He wanted to see if Catherine would marry Samuel.*

I'd rather she marry Samuel than anyone else, Susanna consented to that much. *No wonder Samuel has been around here so much lately. No wonder Catherine's mind is so far away that she forgets what she is doing.*

Susanna's toe had stopped throbbing, and she was getting over the shock. *I thought we four Ulriches would stay together a long time. But Catherine can't stay with us always. I will miss her, but I will still have Grandmother.*

That evening Grandfather loaded a barrel of grain on the wagon, along with the Ulriches and Maria, and he took them to Hans Graf's new mill. They rode up the old Peters Road toward the place where the Cocalico Creek empties into the Conestoga Creek. On the way, Grandfather showed them the trail that went toward the Nageles, Landises, and the men's solitary cabins.

Fulcrum and levering pole.

Later, at a turn in the trail, they heard the sound of a rushing creek. Through the trees they saw the biggest building that Susanna had ever seen. It was made of stone, and Samuel was finishing a wall for the race. Nearby, a new settler by the name of Carpenter and his ox moved a huge rock toward the wall with a fulcrum and levering pole. It moved closer toward Samuel. With a long pole, Samuel glided the perfectly-shaped rock into the wall. When Samuel called loudly, Mr. Carpenter released the rock and Samuel unfastened it.

Grandfather had stopped the wagon at the edge of the Conestoga Creek, and they watched a few more rocks glide into place.

"Hans Graf did well when he hired Samuel and Gabriel to finish the mill. It will be used by the Carpenters and the many new settlers arriving along the Cocalico Creek," Grandfather commented admiringly.

The mill which stood on the south side of the Conestoga Creek was the grandest mill in the Conestoga Valley.

Gabriel came and invited them into the lower room to watch the mill work. When they were all inside, he swung open the window shutter. Reaching out, he pulled a rope and fastened its end to a wooden peg. They heard the water gushing through the opened gate in the mill race.

There was a groan and squeak of wood turning against wood. It rumbled louder and louder until the whole building seemed to shudder. Then Gabriel poured Grandfather's grain into the hopper which directed it into the hole in the upper millstone. The shafts and cogs which were connected to the mill wheel turned the upper stone around on top of the stationary lower stone. Slowly, the meal poured from the stones into Grandfather's wooden barrel.

When Gabriel stopped the mill, it was very quiet. "It isn't perfect," Gabriel said apologetically. "After the wood is worn from usage, it will run smoothly as any wheel."

"That won't take long," Grandfather assured him. "You've done a good job."

Susanna looked at Catherine and Samuel who had just entered the outside door behind them.

Maudlin and Henry Weber's marriage will go as smoothly as a well-worn wheel, Susanna recalled.

When they were alone, Catherine took Susanna's hand. "You heard what Grandfather said about Samuel and me. Do you mind if I marry Samuel?" she asked.

"No, I don't mind, if your marriage will run as smoothly as a well-worn wheel," Susanna replied. "I will miss you, but Grandmother is the best mother we could have had. If only I could know that you'll be truly happy."

"Grandfather's marriage is perfect. With God's help, we want our marriage to run smoothly, also," Catherine assured Susanna.

CHAPTER 12

Mennonite Mayflower

After a dry autumn with numerous forest fires, word came that the ship *Molly* was at sea with 300 Swiss Brethren aboard. Another ship, *William and Sarah*, had left Holland a week ahead of *Molly* and had arrived a long time ago, bringing the Diffenderfers who were Lutherans. The Hubers had helped them to build their cabin on Saeue Schwamm. Now it was November; *Molly* was late.

During the fall, Grandfather had often said, "Let's finish this so that we have time to help the new settlers build their cabins before winter." Sometimes, when they had put extra things away, Catherine was dreamy. Susanna knew those things were for Catherine and Samuel.

One day, near the end of November, Susanna and Maria were helping Grandfather and Jacob get firewood. It was hard work lifting the heavy logs on the sled, even after Grandfather and Jacob had cut them the right length.

"Good wood warms you thrice," Grandfather said, repeating an old saying. "When you cut it, when you burn it, and when you feel the hot embers warming your soul."

Susanna knew it was worth the hard work, not only to assure their warmth next winter, but also to have extra wood to give to the needy.

"Did you know that some of our brethren who arrived back in 1710 have again applied for naturalization?" Jacob asked his father. "Hopefully, our new governor will be more lenient than the last one. Our other petition was refused because of our peculiarity in dress, religion, political ideas, and our German language."

"With more Swiss Brethren coming, our new governor may have new fears about us seizing their government. There are so many of us," Grandfather reminded Jacob, as he paused in chopping firewood. "We don't want them to take our land and send us away like they did in Switzerland and Germany. Holland never allowed us to become citizens either."

Jacob leaned on his ax handle as he said, "Our brethren are cautious when giving the value of their possessions and declaring their religious views. English copies of our Dortrecht Confession accompany their petition. If we wish to buy, sell, or bequeath land to our children, we must become citizens.

"*Molly* is the third ship that will have to furnish a passenger list. Every man and boy on the list must go to the Philadelphia courthouse. There he must declare his allegiance to the King of England." Jacob spoke with concern, "I hope this will not affect our nonresistant stand and our refusal to hold government office."

"Sauer's plea for Mennonites to vote to keep Quakers in office doesn't sound right," his father added critically. "If we are not of this kingdom, why should we vote?"

The men were busy chopping the firewood when Maria called, "Hans Graf is coming!"

They paused to hear the pounding of horses' hoofs and the screech of the wagon wheels. When Graf came into view he called, "Messengers arrived and said that *Molly* was seen in the distance yesterday. We are going to fetch the families. By the way, I saw snow flurries up north yesterday." His wagon was followed by one driven by his son Peter. They drove on by, hoping to get to Philadelphia by tomorrow.

✝ ✝ ✝ ✝

Late one afternoon, Susanna and Maria were gathering any remaining walnuts along Peters Road and were dressed warmly for the cold December weather. Grandfather had gone along to repair fence. There they could listen for the wagons which would bring the new settlers.

Susanna thought about all the preparations that had been made to welcome *Molly*'s passengers.

The evening before, Susanna had stacked shingles as fast as Grandfather could split them. To assure easy splitting, the pine logs had been squared and dried for a year. Water soon leaked through the quickly made bark shingles, so Grandfather wanted to give pine shingles to the new settlers.

Grandfather had held the frow where he wished to strike. The frow was a heavy knife blade with a handle. With the other hand he had struck the blade with a hammer called a maul, and the shingles fell to the ground. Thus each shingle was divided from the log with a single blow.

Susanna had also stacked wood in the cabin. She had placed two forked sticks and a long stick in place at both ends of the high pile to keep it from falling.

In a tree near their cabin, Susanna and Maria had carved a notch for each day of November. One notch was extra deep because that day Susanna had turned twelve. Every day made them more ready to welcome the coming settlers.

Susanna was pleased with the pile of freshly husked corn in the cratch. Watch was tied there to keep away the squirrels.

The floor in the corner of the loft was covered with blocks of soap. Daily Susanna turned each block to assure proper drying. Rows of candles hung from frames. Clusters of round puffed flowers of hop plants hung on the walls to dry. They would be used to brew yeast when they made bread.

Last week three hogs had been butchered. Twice a day Susanna had added hickory wood to the smoldering fire in the smokehouse which was full of meat. Crocks of puddins, which they ate with cornmeal mush, and blocks of scrapple joined the crocks of pork pickling in saltwater. The fresh tenderloins and ribs had been covered with lard to preserve them. Grandmother had collected the fat and wood ashes to make another kettle of soap.

The women had baked three hams, apple pies, and bread for the men who were felling trees and building cabins.

At the first thud of horses' hoofs, Maria and Susanna raced to the corner where the trails met. "Look, there are two wagons, and people walking!" Maria shouted.

Suddenly the girls felt shy; they did not know these people. Three boys, a man, and a young couple waved to them. Henry Weber and Peter Graf also waved from the wagons.

"Welcome to the Conestoga Valley!" Grandfather called from the edge of the trail.

"Brother Hans," the men cried together as they greeted, "it is good to see you!"

Susanna and Maria learned to know Christian Wenger and his new wife, Eve, immediately. Eve was one of Grandfather's cousins. The man with the three boys was David Martin, whose wife died on the sea. David was interested in education and brought his big collection of books along with him.

"Maybe David will be the schoolteacher at Weber Thal next year," Maria suggested after the wagons left.

There was much activity in the following days. One day the men helped at Jacob Bar's cabin-raising on Mill Creek. The following day they hauled the shingles on the sled to Christian Wenger's land and had another cabin-raising. The men fastened the shingles to the roof that night.

☩ ☩ ☩ ☩

Grandfather's wagon was filled with many things as the ox pulled it eastward down the Horseshoe Trail. The group following the wagon walked briskly in the cold air. They counted the deer grazing on Saeue Schwamm. Behind the schwamm the Welsh Mountain stretched as far to the east as the settlers could see.

"The Ebys are helping a black man," Peter informed them. "He escaped from the iron works on French Creek and is hiding in the Welsh Mountain."

"I'd like to see a black person sometime," Maria exclaimed with curiosity.

"They are treated more cruelly than redemptioners," Christopher said sadly.

"Grandfather, what are redemptioners?" Susanna asked.

"When people who arrive on ships don't have money to pay their way, someone pays it for them. In return, the redemptioners work for this person for a certain amount of time. After that, the redemptioners often have difficulty in finding their families."

Later the group followed a branch of the Conestoga Creek into Weber Thal. David Martin and his boys were grateful for the abundant provisions. The remainder of their gifts went to the Sensimans and Schniders, whose three-sided shelters were finished.

Further down the creek they saw three bark wigwams. A woman was shoveling hot embers into an iron kettle. The water in the kettle sizzled and steamed as it turned into lye. Then she added a basket of shelled corn. More steam arose as she stirred with a long pole. After the hulls came off, the corn would become white balls of hominy.

Beside her, another woman was grinding the hominy into grits with a mortar and pestle. On another grate they were roasting corn.

"Indians know how to make so many things from corn," Catherine remarked.

While visiting, they learned that the Brickers, Brubachers, Bombergers, Mussers, Rutts, and Wanners had settled in other places in the Conestoga Valley. Many who were sick had remained in Germantown for the winter.

"Meetings will be started in many new places," Grandfather predicted on the way home. "Soon there will be ordinations for ministers. We've needed a minister since Nagele left. With more people the need is greater."

"Did you hear them call the ship *Molly* the Mennonite *Mayflower*?" Christopher chuckled.

"All these new arrivals should give Beissel some competition. Maybe he'll leave," Peter suggested.

"A Mennonite *Mayflower* will not lessen Conestoga Valley's problems," Grandfather doubted. "More people bring more problems. Beissel is not about to leave. We must rise above him spiritually."

"I hope the Mennonite *Mayflower* will provide us a with a minister," Susanna said.

"I feel certain that it will," Grandfather assured her.

Chapter 13

The Tinder Box

"Grandmother, can you start this fire?" Catherine's voice sounded from below in the main room of the cabin.

"Try the pine chips in the tinder box," Grandmother suggested. "I should have banked the fire last night." Today was wash day. The kettle of water was waiting for Catherine to make a good cooking fire.

Susanna felt warm in her tick in the loft, but suddenly she discovered her face was cold.

"I hope Grandmother allows us to sleep until it is warmer down there," Maria's muffled words came from the tick next to Susanna's. Maria had spent the night at Susanna's house.

"This is January," Susanna reminded Maria. "It's good Grandmother knows how to strike sparks. Catherine is awfully slow."

"You wouldn't be any faster," Maria stated with certainty. "If there were no kindling in the tinder box, we'd have to fetch hot coals from my cabin."

There was a fast clicking of one stick against another and then silence. "Your fire will start now," Grandmother encouraged Catherine. Soon Susanna heard the familiar crackling of burning kindling.

"Time to get up, girls!" Grandmother called.

"Mill Creek has become a real tinder box in the past year," they heard Catherine say as they fluffed their ticks. "So many fires have been started from its dried kindling."

"Catherine is probably talking about the forest fires from last fall," Maria supposed with a loud whisper.

"Indians need to control weeds in their cornfields somehow. The easiest way is to burn this year's seeds." Susanna offered a good reason.

"It isn't only the Indians' fires," Maria insisted. "It is the fires of more than 200 families who have recently settled in the Conestoga Valley."

"Grandfather says there will be a shortage of meat because so many animals have died from the smoke. I'll be happy to breathe good fresh air again," Susanna added with a sniff.

"They say that our only income this year will be from the hemp which goes to Philadelphia," Maria told her. "The extra butter and wheat must stay here to feed these new settlers."

When the girls came downstairs to the fire, Grandmother said more. "Plenty of good things have started here lately, too. Samuel, Israel, Emanuel, and you were so happy on your baptism day, Catherine. Your lives have been changed."

The scene of Bishop Christian Herr pouring water on their heads was vivid in Susanna's mind. The young people were so serious about baptism.

The older people feared the evil influences which Israel Eckerlin had brought with him from Germantown. Hans Graf said that it would take more than a new environment to change Israel. Hans had had a long talk with Israel, which no one seemed to know much about.

A few days later, it was evident to all that Israel was not the same. No longer did they hear bad stories about him. Rather than staying outside during the meetings at Grafs, he came in and worshipped. He supported his leaders and cheered his mother with obedience.

"Yes, the Lord has made us all different than we used to be," Catherine's voice rang with gratefulness. "But, Grandmother, I'm talking about another kind of fire. I'm talking about Beissel's doctrine. It is spreading like fire. I'm worried about Israel. He attended the German Baptists' meetings."

"You mean the meetings at Hildebrands?" Grandmother's quick response filled the air with suspense. "What drew him there?"

"It isn't right!" Catherine aired her concern. "While Israel was repairing a stone wall at the Sauers, Christopher urged him to attend the meetings. Israel refused until Christopher bribed him."

"Sauer knew Israel's past weakness of accepting bribes. How could Sauer stoop to such an act?" Grandmother cried with disappointment. "What did Israel think of the meetings?"

"Israel expected to find anything but purity and holiness there. Instead, Beissel's preaching has stirred his thinking. He feels inflamed with the spirit of the meeting in a way that he can't forget," Catherine replied.

"What does Samuel think of this?" Grandmother wanted to know.

"Samuel can't forget Beissel's unwillingness to provide his share of the food when those men lived with him. The one man still accuses him of dishonesty. Also, Samuel can't respect a man who disrespects his elders."

"Sauer isn't a Baptist himself. Why did he bribe Israel to go to their meetings?" Grandmother reasoned.

"I don't know why, but he might reap the consequences of his actions," Catherine assured Grandmother.

"How?"

"If he won't become a part of some religious group, his wife, Marie, is threatening to join Beissel's group and go into solitude. Beissel says a spiritual person doesn't marry. Some call him a forbidder of marriage."

"What is so good about going into solitude in a little hut by oneself?" Grandmother asked.

"Daniel Eicher's two girls say that the time alone with God in solitude is important in solving their problems," Catherine answered. "They left their parents a year ago and didn't return home."

"Is going into solitude a righteous method of running away?" Grandmother hinted. "Why don't they make restitution, forgive, and go home with their parents? Anna, the oldest, is only eighteen."

"I don't know," Catherine answered. "They are not the sweet, happy girls who attended our meetings. Every time Beissel goes visiting, they and all the brethren follow him. They look like a mob of forsaken, unhappy people dressed in the poorest of Mennonite clothing. I'm ashamed of them."

"Such confusion! Never!" Grandmother cried.

"They are attending Beissel's convent school along Mill Creek," Catherine added. "Beissel asked the Baptist brethren to teach, but they refused, so he is the teacher."

"I wish that we could go to a school like the one that started on Weber Thal," Maria said wistfully.

"Beissel's school is only a mile away, but you'll never be allowed to go there," Grandmother spoke firmly. "We've been told to avoid it."

The pops and sizzling that followed seemed to blend with the moment.

54

"I'd like to go to Christopher Dock's school. Beissel's eyes scare me. I wouldn't want him to teach me," Susanna declared.

"He is too little to hurt anyone," Maria giggled in a whisper.

"The harm he can do is too serious to laugh about," Grandmother rebuked her sternly. "Johannes Hildebrand is threatening to take his family back to Germantown so his daughter can't go into solitude. Beissel's followers are breaking their families' hearts."

Catherine's next words shocked her listeners. "In the afternoon on Christmas Day, everyone is invited to the baptism of the Eicher girls and four others. They have a love feast at dinner time. Anna Eicher is begging Aunt Anna to attend their baptism. Aunt Anna wants to go into solitude."

"Not Aunt Anna!" Susanna and Maria gasped together.

"Whatever does my daughter see in Beissel?" Grandmother cried in alarm.

Pop! There was a loud hissing. Another pop followed with hissing and sizzling. To heat the wash water faster, Catherine dropped each hot rock into the pot of water. The pops and sizzling that followed seemed to blend in with the moment.

"The talk about the Eicher girls and Beissel isn't very good," Catherine went on. "They are infatuated with him. He visits their cabin too much."

"I can't understand Marie Sauer," Grandmother sounded puzzled. "When I bought sewing needles from her, she was against Beissel. Now she wants to follow him."

"How did Marie manage to bring sewing needles to America to sell?" Susanna asked.

"She brought them in her tick," Grandmother informed her.

Maria sniffed the frying *pon haus*. "Breakfast smells good," she remarked. "With no *pon haus* to eat, Marie Sauer will get thin. Beissel says it is wrong to eat meat."

"The Bible says it is good to eat meat," Catherine argued. "I'm going to stay a Mennonite, get married, and eat meat."

"Beissel is the tinder box; his doctrine is the kindling. Every time someone strikes their stick with his, another fire is kindled," Grandmother figured aloud. "Conestoga Valley will soon be a boiling pot if all that you say is true."

CHAPTER 14

Dumb Dutchman

"You say he is hiding above where the water flows upstream!" the angered Irishman shouted. "Ha! Ha! So you, Mr. Eby, you dumb Dutchman, would have me to believe such a tale! If I ever find my runaway slave with you, you'll be sorry."

Susanna was relieved when the owner of the iron foundry at French Creek mounted his horse and rode away.

Theodorus Eby calmly emptied the next customer's grain into the hopper.

The words, "where the water flows upstream," rang in Susanna's ears. Then she remembered. Her brother Peter had taken their calf to a settler who lived above where the water flows upstream. Where is that? Water flows downstream.

Christopher Sauer, also in the Eby's Mill that morning, rubbed his hand back and forth over his flowing white beard as he always did when he had something important to say. The room full of Germans waited to see what this gentleman, who was usually calm, was thinking.

"Why must English-speaking people call German-speaking people dumb Dutchmen?" he began. "We brought with us our German Bibles, prayer books, confessions of faith, psalteries, works of Menno Simons, and our *Ausbunds*. Most of us can read them. Every Dutchman's shelf has more than one book beside the almanac. Germans read more in German than the English read in English. English books are hard to find. How can we learn English with no English to read?"

"Sauer, why are you soaking rags in water barrels on the back side of the creek?" a newcomer challenged him.

I never saw him before. What will Sauer say? Susanna asked herself.

Sauer avoided the stranger's question and spoke more of his own thoughts.

56

"Reason a bit. We dumb Dutchmen, whether we be Baptist, Mennonite, or Lutheran, read and write from our Bibles in High German. We speak our own German dialect. Also, many of us speak one Indian dialect. The Grafs speak a number of Indian dialects. We are all slow at learning English, our fourth language, but where is the Englishman who knows any tongue but English?"

Susanna knew that she could converse with Quick Foot's family. She also talked with the Indians who came to sell their hickory brooms and willow whip baskets.

"Think further," Sauer went on. "Who is starting schools in Penn's Woods? Christopher Dock and Francis Pastorius are not teaching in the dark down east. Neither do the Mennonite schools in Pequea teach at night."

"Amen," the room of settlers agreed audibly.

"Who makes the only, and much sought after, paper in Penn's Woods?" Sauer asked. "Even the governments of other colonies pay a great price for it."

"Three Germans in Philadelphia who see a need for paper," a man replied.

"And find an Englishman who will stoop to the lowly task of making paper."

"The only paper most of us have is the back of a hard-to-find calendar," John Diffenderfer exclaimed with a laugh.

"We haven't forgotten how to write on shingles with a charcoal bit," Daniel Eicher added.

"Sometimes, we have reasons for not learning English," Sauer suggested. "At one English tavern the sign says, 'The best food in town.' The English tavern further down the road says, 'The best food in the world.' Many German taverns have no sign at all. Do we want our children to learn how to blow their horn as the English do? The reward one has for having done his best is sufficient," Sauer concluded as he reached for his bag of meal and departed.

"When they call us dumb Dutchmen, let us take it patiently, lest someday they take our freedom," Theodorus quietly warned those who remained.

The red-faced stranger who had challenged Sauer slipped out the door.

✣ ✣ ✣ ✣

"Where does water flow upstream?" Susanna asked Catherine on their way home from the mill.

"I'm not sure, but there is a place like that," Catherine replied.

"Who lives there? Who has our calf?" Susanna prompted her.

"Your guess is as good as mine," Catherine answered, uninterested.

"Why is Sauer soaking rags in water?" Susanna wondered.

"It is a part of making paper," Catherine explained. "Grandfather has seen other things which make him certain that Sauer is making a printing press. Jacob Gass, one of Beissel's followers, is helping to do it. Perhaps some day it will be legal for Sauer to print Bibles in German. We must not talk about Sauer's doings in public. It could give him trouble. We wish that every home could have a Bible. Bibles from Europe are expensive."

"You will not have a Bible when you get married," Susanna reminded Catherine. "The only Bibles we have are the ones Grandfather and Grandmother and other parents brought with them."

"I'm glad that Grandmother taught us to write. She has such colorful fraktur written on their marriage certificate," Catherine commented.

"Yes, and the doves on it are beautiful," Susanna added. She looked at Catherine closely and asked, "Are you getting married soon?"

"Don't ask me how soon," Catherine replied. "It will be hard for me to leave you, little sister." She set her bag of meal on the ground to talk.

"Help me get the flax pulled and ready for watering and knot your stockings for this winter. Then, I will help you decorate one of my crocks for your thirteenth birthday."

"The crocks, pie plates, and vinegar jug that Samuel gave to you are beautiful," Susanna exclaimed. "And the pitcher with the tulip design is perfectly shaped."

"He fired his kiln on a very hot day last July so the crockery would cool more gradually. Our pottery should not break easily because he fired it six times," Catherine explained.

"When are you going to paint your pottery?" Susanna wondered.

"When I find gum on the cherry trees, I'll dilute it with water and use that to preserve the colors. I've burned grapevine twigs for the black; berries from poke weed will make red; and saffron will make yellow," Catherine shared her enthusiasm. "Yes, and boiled down walnut hulls that have been mashed first have made a perfect brown. I made blue out of the indigo that Hans Graf brought from Philadelphia."

"What will you write in the circle between the tulips?" Susanna asked her.

"Anyone can plant a flower. To give it fragrance, only God has the power," Catherine answered. "Some people think the love of worldly beauty is wrong. Grandmother's needle work and the painting on her cupboard and pie plates reveal her love of beauty. I want our new home to be like that."

Susanna caught herself becoming eager to see Catherine's new home.

"When you read the Bible and prayer book to Grandmother as she works, think about what you're reading," Catherine reminded her. "When Grandfather and our brothers read the Bible, cherish it. When you sing songs from the *Ausbund* on winter nights and on Sundays, sing with all your heart. It will make life more meaningful."

"So we are dumb Dutchmen!" Susanna smiled.

"Maybe we are *called* dumb Dutchmen, but we need not *be* dumb Dutchmen," Catherine decided. "It doesn't matter so much what they *say* we are, but what we are. If we live right and are kind, they might finally admit that we aren't dumb."

Chapter 15

Sudden Solitude

Susanna and her brothers sat quietly around the table waiting for Jacob Huber to come. He was coming to hear Grandfather talk about something important. Susanna knew something was amiss by the looks on Grandfather's and Grandmother's faces. So much good had happened lately. What could be wrong?

>Susanna remembered well the Sunday morning in March when Catherine married Samuel Eckerlin. It had happened during the meeting at Grafs on the day which she and her brothers had predicted it would be.
>Now Catherine lived in Samuel's well-built cabin under the nut trees where Peters Road and Horseshoe Trail met. Catherine and Samuel were happy. Susanna did not mind the short walk to their cabin.
>Susanna also remembered vividly Christian Wenger's ordination in April. Since then, he had preached one Sunday at Grafs and the next at Carpenters. The Wengers had built a stone house with an oak floor and small windows. They had an iron heating stove. Christian's sister Elizabeth worked for them. She and Catherine were the same age and good friends.
>Ten more cabins had been raised on Saeue Schwamm. All of the families had attended meetings at Grafs, but now they held Lutheran meetings in their own homes.
>Some of their surnames were Smith, Miller, Schmidt, Witmer, Hoffman, Keyser, and the Kochs, who were Grandmother's relatives. Susanna could

see their cluster of homes from the Hubers' cabin. Their chimneys rose at the end of the roof. The Mennonites built chimneys in the center of their cabins to conserve heat.

Crowds of new settlers had been coming to the meeting at Grafs. There were the Rudys, Stauffers, Millers, and Musselmans. The minister preached from the doorway so that those remaining outside could hear.

Hans Graf's mill was convenient for the newcomers arriving in the Carpenter area and up the Cocalico Creek. Gabriel Eckerlin was running the mill. His brothers, Israel and Samuel, were building Christian Wenger's barn.

Life was good in the Conestoga Valley. Neighbors helped each other. Beissel was fading into the background—or so they thought.

Samuel and Christian had talked of starting a school. Susanna always became excited at the thought of school. Maybe she could go to school before she turned fourteen, she hoped.

The seriousness of the moment rested upon Susanna as Jacob entered the cabin and sat down with his parents and the Ulrichs.

After what seemed like a long time, Grandfather began to speak. "I have sad news to tell you that is going to affect all Conestoga Valley. On Whit Sunday, Israel, Jacob Gass, and four others will be rebaptized by Beissel.

"Beissel's new pamphlet on the Sabbath Day is circulating everywhere. His congregation has adopted the Sabbath Day for divine services. They will work six days and rest on the seventh. At every meeting, one after the other of his followers revolts against his seventh-day worship or his teachings on marriage. At such a time, Israel plans to join Beissel and build himself a hut in the wilderness.

"Anna Eckerlin's heart is broken over this. She knew that Israel had been with Beissel's followers lately, but she thought that her son was content to be a Mennonite. All day Israel has been trying to assure her that all will be well. Samuel says that he won't last long in solitude. He likes people too much.

"Israel wishes to be alone and to find God's will for his life. Mennonite meetings seem too formal for him. He feels a call to do things which he cannot do in the Mennonite Church."

"Samuel warned Israel that Beissel's beliefs are contrary to the Scriptures. Israel insisted that he would not be following Beissel entirely."

"I don't always spend enough time alone with God either, but I don't have to go into solitude to correct it," Jacob reasoned.

"Our formal Mennonite meetings feed the soul more than the pietistic meetings that my family attended," Grandmother shared.

"Israel can't wait for his call to preach to come through our church. Beissel supports self-appointed preachers," Jacob informed them. "The scriptural way is for church leaders to ordain leaders of proper age."

"Jacob Gass will continue working with Sauer on the printer," Grandfather went on. "They hope, in time, to produce a German Bible."

"Who of us will read a Bible coming from their hands?" Peter contended. "Further, it is illegal to print German Bibles in an English country."

"We need Bibles badly," Grandfather reminded Peter. "Catherine and Samuel come here when they wish to read the Scriptures. Perhaps we should thank God that a Bible is going to be printed."

"I hope no one follows Israel," Peter exclaimed.

"We older people see Beissel as having a sorry mixture of teaching, which produced church squabbles in Europe," Grandfather told them. "Israel is confused. Beissel is a very persuasive person, and he will have followers.

"I do not want any of you to discuss religious matters with him or any follower of Beissel. Meditation so that the Spirit can speak without acceptance of scriptural and church leaders' authority opens one to all kinds of error. Only the Spirit's direction under proper authority provides safe guidance. Let us pray."

They knelt and Grandfather prayed like Susanna never heard him pray before. He thanked God for truth and for faithful Mennonite leaders. Then he asked God to keep each of them safe from the false doctrines about them. He entreated God to keep Catherine and Samuel and all of the other Eckerlins from Israel's persuasive power.

When they arose from their knees, Susanna noticed a look of calmness and rest on Grandfather's face. All appeared to have unloaded their burdens. It seemed as if God's protective arm was wrapped tightly about them.

Susanna's mouth watered for the broken pieces of sugar which she would carry back home for supper.

Chapter 16

The Boiling Pot

Susanna pushed more wood into the fire under the large kettle of steaming sap. Grandfather kept stirring the thickening maple syrup.

Christopher had planned and worked for what he called the Ulrich sugaring. Last May, when the trees livened with new sap, he had cut six-foot poles from hickory saplings. Hickory trees grew plentiful around Saeue Schwamm. Then he had tied the poles in bundles and soaked them in the small stream below the spring house. These he would use to make buckets.

After a long soaking, the poles were pounded with a mallet and then split into long strips. Next, Christopher fastened the strips to staves and hooked the ends of the strips together to form a bucket. When the strips had dried, the buckets were tight and sturdy. Quick Foot insisted that they would never wear out.

During the winter Quick Foot had helped Christopher hollow out the centers of sumac stems with a hot rod. The spout was then pushed into the tree trunk through a hole which they had hollowed out with a knife. Now, after four days of warm weather, the sap was flowing. The buckets which he had fastened to the sugar maples were almost full.

That morning Peter and Christopher had loaded Grandfather's barrels on the sled barrow and skidded it across the melting snow to the sugar maples. All morning they had emptied the buckets of sap into the barrels. When the barrels were full, they slid

> them to the iron kettles which Peter had hung from strong poles.

Susanna's mouth watered for the broken pieces of sugar which she would carry back home for supper.

When the kettles were full, she tended the fires while the others stirred.

"Conestoga Valley has become a boiling pot since Israel went into solitude," Jacob commented as he chopped wood for the fire. "This boiling sap reminds me of the fires which Beissel has fed."

> Soon after Israel Eckerlin had gone into solitude, the community rose up against Beissel's group for working on Sunday. They took advantage of them in every way imaginable. Finally, the civil authorities reminded them of the English law which said that they should not work on Sunday. They replied that they regarded God's law more than England's law.
>
> Beissel was not happy with his people's behavior. When the next ones had been summoned to court, Beissel prayed for them, and the authorities dismissed them in peace. Beissel said that God had given the hearts of the authorities into his hand. After that, his followers paid their fines, and the authorities relaxed their strictness.

"As Samuel predicted, Israel didn't stay in solitude very long," Peter reminded them. "He declared that he would have lost his mind if he had stayed longer."

"Why did Israel move his mother and brothers to Jan Neily's cabin?" Christopher asked.

"We can only guess what Israel is scheming," Grandfather replied. "Israel should be feeling responsibile for his mother. Instead, he leaves on an evangelistic trip as a self-appointed preacher. Jan's cabin is conveniently close to the sisters' solitary cabins. Anna Eckerlin is weary of the sisters' daily visits. She sent Gabriel to the Wengers to remove him from their influence. At the other place, Catherine and Veronica lived nearby and assisted her. Now the sisters help her against her wishes."

"Since Anna is gone, the Eicher girls are more free in visiting Catherine and Veronica. They will convince them yet," Jacob told Grandfather. "They've also persuaded Jacob Grafs to attend Beissel's meetings again. All the while, Jan has been indoctrinating Samuel."

"If Catherine and Veronica go into solitude, who will care for Veronica's children? And who will care for Catherine and her little one that will arrive soon?" Grandfather cried. "The life of a lone parent is difficult in the Conestoga Valley. Didn't we care well enough for Veronica? Will she turn against us?"

"Veronica is tired of being a burden to the Mennonites. This way she can grow spiritually and care for herself, and a householder family will be parents to her children," Jacob told them. "Children in the convent are kept by one parent or a householder. Catherine will care for her baby."

"What is a householder?" Susanna asked.

"Beissel's followers who do not live in celibacy are called householders," Jacob explained.

"Would it be right for Catherine to leave Samuel?" Christopher asked.

"It would be wrong! It sounds sick and ridiculous," Jacob exclaimed. "Most of Beissel's followers are Mennonites. He will take more of us if we let him."

"If God could settle Hans Graf's problems through our leaders, He can work out Catherine's and Veronica's problems, too," Grandfather insisted.

"What does Gabriel think?" Jacob asked Grandfather.

"Gabriel does not wish to go with Beissel. He respects his mother's wishes, and our brethren are trying to help him."

"Beissel's doctrine might destroy us," Jacob declared. "It is more frightful than the painted Conestoga Indians who stalked by here. That was a threat to all of Conestoga Valley. They were on their way to repay the Shawnees for killing a Conestoga man and woman. We were thankful that the Shawnees didn't retaliate."

"What can stop Israel's bad influence?" Christopher wondered. "On his way to Germantown he stops to visit someone on Weber Thal."

"Philip Holty, who arrived on the ship *Morton House*, said that Israel meets young men as they come off the ships," Peter added. "He invites them to his meetings and gets them stirred with his doctrine. Philip attended one meeting, but after talking with Bishop

Rittenhouse, he never returned. He had to avoid Israel to get rid of him."

Suddenly, Susanna cried out, "Why do such terrible things happen to us?"

Susanna felt Grandfather's hand on her shoulder. "I'm sorry, children, that this has happened to you. Your disappointment will be for a time. Then God will say, 'it is enough.' His mercy will not leave you suffer more than you can bear."

"Grandfather, my syrup is turning to sugar," Peter said after a long silence when tears were dried.

"It is time to empty the kettle. We can find enjoyment in this if we leave our troubles with God who understands," Grandfather said, tenderly. With the nipper he cut off a lump of sugar for each of them.

His words comforted Susanna. She knew this day of the Ulrich sugaring would never be forgotten.

CHAPTER 17

Den Of Serpents

All too soon Grandfather's fears for Samuel and Catherine Eckerlin were realized. To their dismay, they learned that Samuel was living alone near the men. He was building a cabin for Catherine in the sisters' convent.

Soon afterward, Catherine's baby was born dead. She wept, but felt more than ever that she should remain where she was. Samuel came to bury his son, but then left again.

Susanna cried when she saw the tiny face in the linen shroud. "Now he won't need to grow up without parents to care for him," she thought. She was ready to accept what Grandmother had agreed was best.

Veronica Eberly and her children planted a garden to supply enough food for the coming year. Had she given up her strange notion to go into solitude?

✢ ✢ ✢ ✢

In July, Veronica's oldest son, Jacob, visited Grandfather Huber. Susanna was there and heard Jacob say, "Mother still talks about going to the convent and sending us to the Nageles."

"How does this make you feel?" Grandfather asked the troubled young man before him.

"Not very happy," Jacob replied. "Emanuel Eckerlin is going into solitude. He has built a cabin in the den of snakes and wants me to live with him."

"Where is his cabin?" Grandfather asked.

"It is at Koch-Halekung near where the stream from the watering place flows into the Cocalico Creek. Quick Foot says the Indians avoid the place because its meadow and banks are infested with snakes."

Who would want to live in a snake pit by himself? I'm glad my brothers stay at home, Susanna decided to herself.

"Is it right that my mother does not care for us?" Jacob inquired with a look of defiance. "Was it right for my father to send us to America alone?"

"It makes you want to hate them, doesn't it?" Grandfather replied calmly. "It's not right, but the Bible says children are to honor and obey their parents. You should do this even though your parents do wrong."

"I can't do that! Father didn't love us, and Mother doesn't either," Jacob insisted.

"I understand," Grandfather spoke with sympathy. "You need to come and tell me these things. If your mother forsakes you and your brothers and sisters, you come here. You may live with us as long as you do not follow Beissel."

"Never will I follow him," Jacob declared. "I want to be a Mennonite like you. Emanuel didn't like it that Gabriel was at Wengers, so he left home. Now Gabriel has had to go home to care for his mother."

"Show your love and faithfulness to your mother. God can help you," Grandfather admonished Jacob.

"Thank you. If Mother leaves us, we will come to you, and I will work hard to pay you for it."

"I know you will. You are a worker," Grandfather said as he looked affectionately at the robust fourteen-year-old before him.

Yes, he is a hardworking, thrifty Eberly. Susanna understood what Grandfather saw in Jacob. *But, will it come to all this,* she wondered.

By now Beissel's followers were divided into three groups. Most of the celibate brethren lived in cabins on Nagele's farm. The spiritual virgins lived in cabins near Jan Neily's place. Those who remained married were called householders. There were sixty cabins scattered about the area for those who lived a solitary life.

Daily the spiritual virgins, and anyone interested, fled to the convent for spiritual food from Beissel. There, wonderful influence from heaven came upon them, but these powers didn't impress everyone.

Susanna missed Catherine because they were not allowed to visit together.

"These wilderness places are disappearing fast," Grandfather told Grandmother after Jacob Eberly left. "Did you hear about the meeting at the Indian wigwam in Hickorytown?"

"I didn't," Grandmother replied, "but I remember the wigwam near the big hickory tree not far from the spring. The cabins in town seemed to crowd in around it. Near the wigwam was the tavern of John Postlewaite."

"Recently the council met with the Indians under the hickory tree and decided to call Hickorytown, Lancaster," Grandfather informed her. "The authorities want to have law and order. Every March, on the first day, we must pay one English silver shilling in Lancaster."

"The idea of paying taxes is painful because of the unreasonable taxes we paid in Europe," Grandmother exclaimed. "A good government needs this, but I hope they will be fair and continue to give us freedom. But what does that have to do with the wilderness disappearing?"

"On June 9, they held the first courthouse meeting at Postlewaite's Tavern," Grandfather answered. "They established and named seventeen townships in Lancaster County. We live in Earl Township. They're honoring Hans Graf by using his English name, Earl. Our Lutheran and Catholic neighbors give him more honor here than he would have received by killing Anabaptists in Switzerland."

"Hans deserves his reward," Grandmother said respectfully.

"The establishment of counties was necessary because of the increase of settlers," Grandfather continued. "Hans Graf's mill is on the southeastern corner of Warwick Township. Settlers are moving closer to Emanuel Eckerlin. He will not be left alone for long."

"He won't always be there. Probably he'll want to preach," Grandmother reminded him. "Is the new Mennonite meetinghouse near Lancaster completed?"

"Yes, the oak plank benches are made. Meetings are being held."

"Let's visit there sometime," she suggested.

I'd like to see Lancaster, Susanna dreamed silently.

☩   ☩   ☩   ☩

One day in August, Catherine came to see Jacob's new baby, Catherine, while Susanna was also visiting.

"She is named after you, Catherine, so you remember to come home. You didn't go to the convent intending to stay, did you?" Jacob's wife said hopefully.

"You may as well stay here at home," Jacob pleaded with her.

"I almost came back the other day," Catherine told them, "but that day, young Minister Jacob Weber's wife returned to the convent. The next day, Elizabeth Wenger arrived. She said Aunt Anna is finally coming, too."

"Aunt Anna and Elizabeth are going into the convent?" Susanna almost shrieked.

"Maybe we should put up a fight to get you home," Jacob proposed.

"That would go against your conscience," Catherine reminded Jacob.

"Are you saying that I should not fight to get you and my sister out of that place?" Jacob cried in defense. "My sister will not go there."

"Send her to the Wengers until she is settled," Catherine suggested.

"Israel was building Wengers' barn when he left. How will they help Anna if Elizabeth left? Who is safe anywhere? Catherine, you need to come home," Jacob begged.

"It is my calling to stay there and persuade Elizabeth and Weber's young wife to leave," Catherine insisted. "They will never leave without my help because of the pressure placed on them."

"But you might be there a long time," Jacob's wife warned Catherine.

"I might die there, but what does a young married woman who is separated from her husband do with her life in this wilderness? Will you build a row of Mennonite cabins for us?" Catherine cried in dejection.

"Yes, and you could help others like Magdelena Graf does," Jacob offered.

"I will die a Mennonite. Don't worry about me," she cried after she had held Baby Catherine close for a while. "How can a mother leave her children?" she wept aloud.

"This is not God's plan for you," Jacob reproved Catherine. "You have defied God's chosen leaders in following self-made ministers. You have defied God's Word in following false teachings. You have broken your marriage vows in pretense of finding something more spiritual. Repent of your sin, flee error, and others will follow."

Catherine shrank at Jacob's sternness. Susanna thought she might stay, but suddenly Catherine turned and fled toward the convent. At the edge of the clearing she paused to wave.

"She is so thin lately. She may die there," Jacob's wife cried in grief.

"My dear sister!" Susanna sobbed as she ran up to Horseshoe Trail. Her feathered friends took flight as she stumbled further and further away from home. Finally, she flung herself on the mossy carpet.

Where is the bit of heaven or elysian dale that Hans Graf talked about? Doesn't God care about us? Can't God tell people to leave the solitary life? Why doesn't Beissel die, rather than Catherine's innocent baby? Heavenly Father, can't You hear us orphans and the Eberly children, who may as well be orphans? Must Emanuel live in a den of serpents to find God?

Then she remembered how Grandfather had said that God allows no more suffering than one can bear. Her tears stopped as she decided to go home and be brave.

God will help me bear it if Catherine dies in the convent, she consoled herself.

CHAPTER *18*

The Runaways

Maria was staying with the Hubers to help with the apple picking. Aunt Anna was still helping Eve Wenger.

The apples were perfect. In the spring when Grandfather had cleaned soot from the chimney, it was time to soot apple trees. Susanna had mixed a bucket of soot and a half bucket of ashes and had poured it on the ground in the windward direction of each tree. The next rain soaked it with water, and gas ascended into the trees and killed the insects.

Today they picked apples. Carefully they grasped each apple by the stem and placed it in the straw-filled crate which Grandfather held up to them. After supper they stacked the crates, full of untouched apples, in the ground cellar. Those choice apples would be eaten next spring when the other apples were gone.

Tomorrow they planned to pick the next best apples to store in the ground cellar, also. Grandmother would dry many of them on grass-woven racks which hung above the fireplace. Susanna was hungry for a schnitz pie.

The remaining apples would be gathered and dumped into Grandfather's sled. Then the ox would pull them to Graf's mill to be pressed into cider.

If only Aunt Anna were here to make vinegar, Susanna wished. She shrank from the idea of dividing the rubbery "mother" into each barrel of cider, but it would be her task.

What will Grandfather and Grandmother do with the abundance of apples this year? she wondered. Little did she realize how soon this question would be answered.

The light from the fireplace flickered on the cabin walls about them. Grandmother had sewn cloth bags together for pillows. About them was a collection of several years' worth of goose feathers. Every other year Grandmother plucked the feathers from their ten geese. After they filled each bag with feathers, they would sew the end of the bag shut. Grandfather seemed to have plenty of everything put back for whomever would need it.

After Grandfather finished reading his Bible, he began sharing the day's news. "Thomas Edwards, one of the most important men in the colonial assembly, walked barefoot from his home on Saeue Schwamm to Lancaster. He sat shoeless through the Justice Court sessions."

"Important people don't go barefooted like we commoners do. That's quite a humble beginning," Grandmother laughed.

"They placed the boundaries of Earl Township on a map," Grandfather continued. "Peters Road divides Earl and Leacock Townships. Saeue Schwamm has been given the name Earltown—the largest town in the Conestoga Valley. It is larger than Lancaster.

"They're allowing 109 Germans who came between 1700 and 1710 to become citizens. They praise them for contributing to the enlargement of the British Empire. Also, the Germans improved the wheat for the European markets. They have behaved themselves religiously and peaceably."

"Their talk about us is different than it used to be," Grandmother commented.

"Hans Graf and Christopher Sauer are on the list," Grandfather added. "Maybe we'll feel more secure after some of us are citizens."

A loud clattering of acorns on the shingled roof and children's voices alerted them. A little one cried in the forest. Grandfather sprang toward the door with the rest of them behind him.

From the darkness appeared Quick Foot and the Eberly children. "I brought some runaways," Quick Foot announced hesitantly.

Quickly, Grandmother took the four-year-old Ulrich Eberly to the hearth for warmth. His sobs subsided as his sisters crowded around them, pleading for comfort.

"This morning Mother heard the last of the acorns falling and decided to go to the convent," Ulrich's older brother Jacob explained. "She wants to live on acorns this winter. She took us to the Nageles to be cared for. While they were milking their cows, we decided to come here. None of us wish to be raised in any of Beissel's householders' homes. We gathered our clothes and went to Quick Foot's cabin. He didn't want to bring us until I told him what you had said."

"I wasn't going to take them back to Nageles," Quick Foot made it clear, "but I will return and tell the Nageles what has happened."

"Anna Eckerlin is dying," Jacob said sadly. "Gabriel is the only son that stands by her. He asked Christian Wenger to go for Emanuel. Hans Graf went for Samuel and Israel, who are preaching at Oley."

Grandfather and Quick Foot shook their heads solemnly.

"They plan to pound acorns into flour for porridge, bread, and a hot drink," Quick Foot remarked. "Acorns contain all the nourishment that a man needs, but we need more important things in life than an oak tree. The Indian way is to live close to nature, but only repentance and submission to God and His church bring real peace."

That night, Anna Henderson Eckerlin died. The next day she was buried in Hans Graf's family graveyard along Peters Road. Christian Wenger and Martin Graf gave her last rites. A faithful sister was laid to rest while Gabriel mourned. Anna's other children said nothing.

Emanuel returned to his cabin which was nestled between two wood-crowned hills. From the never-failing spring next to his cabin, a beautiful stream rippled down to the Cocalico Creek, which wound eastward through meadows and around hills where no people lived as yet.

"Why does Mother run away from us?" little Ulrich Eberly often asked. "Does Mother cry and think of us as she gathers acorns?"

"I'm sure she does," Grandmother answered. "Your Father in heaven also loves and knows all about you." Susanna's tears came as she heard these words. She worked hard so that Grandmother could spend more time with Ulrich.

Jacob Eberly and Maria Huber talked together as they picked apples. Jacob was sure that Maria understood him as well as Grandfather. "If only God would keep our parents at home to care for us, things would be different," Jacob blurted out one day.

"God does not force men. He leaves man to make his own choices," Grandfather reminded Jacob.

"If I had children, I would never run away from them," Jacob declared.

"Aunt Anna says that she will never follow Beissel. He is a witch," Maria informed them. "Alexander Mack, the founder of the German Baptists in Europe, arrived last month. On his first meeting with Beissel's followers, the people told him that Beissel was standing beside him, but Alexander could not see him. Only a witch can make himself invisible."

Later, when the Eberly children were outside, Grandfather told Grandmother about the scene at Grandmother Eckerlin's death bed. Susanna heard him as she worked. Grandmother warned them that Beissel would claim their possessions and leave them with nothing. Worse yet, Satan would claim their souls in a false religion that is against marriage and eating meat. On the Judgment Day, they would be wanting for refusal to submit to the Scriptures.

"Anna died, gasping for breath and praying for her sons. Catherine and Gabriel held her hands tightly in those last moments, and for once, not a word of argument was heard. The others stood by helplessly. They had no comfort to offer except to submit, and they would not."

"The Eckerlin boys won't appreciate Beissel's extreme views of simplicity for long," Grandmother predicted. "They appear well fed; but, in spite of God's blessing of abundance of food at the love feasts, Beissel and the rest of them look increasingly malnourished. Who eats the remaining food in the overflowing vessels at the end of the feasts? Out of concern, we give them most of that food. There are plenty of leftovers, but still, they remain underfed."

"The Eckerlins want a more reasonable way of life," Grandfather agreed. "Recently, Beissel returned home to find a splendid feather bed in his room. The Eckerlins smiled when he slept on it that night. To their dismay, the next morning the feather bed stood outside his cabin, and his hard sleeping bench was back in its place. Their differences will finally bring difficulties."

"In the meantime, we will find joy in helping their runaways," Grandmother said sadly.

Chapter 19

Swift Waters

It had rained. Snow was melting. Every creek was pouring its waters into the Susquehanna River, filling it to the brim.

"It is too wet to work in the fields. Maybe tomorrow the Graf boys can work on their mill," Grandfather remarked.

It was Sunday morning. The Hubers and Ulrichs were going to Sunday meeting at Grafs. Susanna noticed that the mill wheel was in place, ready to go. Jacob Huber and his sons peered expectantly into the newly dug pond which emptied into the mill race.

"Grandfather, already there are frogs in this pond," one of the boys called.

"Nature soon takes over a man-made pond," Grandfather reminded them.

As the group neared the Graf cabin, they saw Peter Bezellion, the French trader. He and the Indians had slept in Martin Graf's barn. Bezellion often traveled with the Grafs. It was soon learned that Bezellion and some Delaware Indians from Brandywine Creek were traveling together. The Grafs were with them. Bezellion and the Indians were going up the Susquehanna and west to the Ohio Valley, and then on to the Illinois settlement.

"That sounds exciting!" Maria whispered to Susanna. "Let's go along and persuade Bezellion to raft us down the Ohio River into the Mississippi River, and on down to New Orleans. He knows about all those places."

"And sail west to the Santa Fe Trail, and then go by horse to the Santa Fe settlement," Susanna laughed.

Travel was slow because of the mud and swollen creeks. Some of the brethren were discussing the large crate of books which Bezellion had brought for Christopher Sauer.

"Sauer has his first paper for sale," someone informed them. "The rags in his water trough have turned into pulp, and the pulp has been processed through his papermill."

"Now we won't need to go to Germantown for paper," Feronica told the girls. "Mother said if we save every rag, maybe we can afford enough paper to write a letter. If I learn to write fraktur perfectly on a slate, I can have one piece of paper."

"Jacob Grafs are here. There is Priscum," Susanna alerted Maria.

Susanna ran to greet Priscum. "It has been months since we've seen you," she cried.

"I know," Priscum replied. "My parents are so taken up with Beissel that we never come here anymore. They are homesteaders. I hope they don't leave us like Veronica left her children."

"We all have grandparents who will take us," Susanna assured her.

Priscum nodded her head with understanding.

"How did you cross the Conestoga Creek this morning?" Susanna asked.

"We crossed yesterday and slept at Grandmother's house last night. This morning it sounded like the Conestoga Creek was overflowing."

"Come, girls," Christian Wenger called. "You will want to hear what Peter Graf has to say. The meeting will soon begin."

Soon everyone gathered around Peter. Peter Bezellion stood beside him.

"Go ahead," Christian urged Peter.

He is very subdued, Susanna thought, as the broad-shouldered youth stood there looking down.

Slowly, Peter Graf spoke. "I thank God for sparing my life. I thank my father who willingly risked his own life for me. Father and I were returning from Philadelphia with a load of blankets. Because of the heavy rain, we knew that the Brandywine Creek was rising. We traveled quickly, not wishing to be stranded for days on the east side. The eastern fork of the Brandywine was high, but the horses waded through without difficulty. We were anxious about how it was on the west fork.

"As we neared its roaring waters, we met Peter Bezellion and his Indian friends. Many times we had met with difficulties in crossing those high waters. The Indians, who lived along the east fork and knew the creek well, suggested the eddy on the opposite shore as a safe landing place."

Susanna knew an eddy was a place where the water from a smaller creek emptied into the larger creek. There, as the waters met, the current was not as swift.

"I felt myself alone in the strongest current I had ever experienced."

"We followed them above the landing spot," Peter went on. "The Indians each found a short log to hold on to, should they need to float. They crawled on top of Bezellion's wagon and waited to go. Bezellion checked the harnesses and mounted his horse. For a moment he paused to look at the fast-moving current. Then he slapped the reins and his lead horse jerked forward into the water. Not far from shore the horses lost their footing so they had to swim.

"The wagon floated behind as the Indians grasped its sides. Gracefully, the lead horse lead the way through the swift waters. When their feet touched the ground, they eased the wagon safely to shore. The Indians jumped from the wagon and clapped their hands with thankfulness. Father and his horse were by my side.

"'Do you wish to try it, Peter?' Father asked.

"Never had I gone through such high waters before, but if Bezellion could do it, then I would do it, too.

"'Yes, Father, I'll go the same way that they went,' I answered cautiously.

"'I'm behind you if you need help,' Father assured me, 'but you need not go if you are afraid.'"

Susanna knew Hans Graf never forced his boys into dangerous places. Peter was careful, but he was brave, too.

Peter continued, "As my team began to swim, King, my lead horse, lost control. The rest of the team struggled in confusion. When we reached the eddy, we were still in the strongest part of the current. Suddenly, the flow of water from the small creek was too swift. I saw a large whirlpool and felt it pulling us down into its center. There was an instant pull away from it as the horses sensed the danger. Slowly, we gained distance toward the main current, but the wagon leaned over on its side. The whirling water gulped up the blankets in a moment. My horse made an unexpected tug forward, and I felt myself alone in the strongest current I had ever experienced. I gasped for breath—and remember no more.

"Then, I felt strong hands pushing down on me. Water was being forced from my nose and mouth. I gasped for breath as Father's voice, which sounded far away, cried, 'Peter, breathe!!' Father continued to press down on me and after many gasps, I was finally able to breathe on my own. The Indians gave me hot tea and wrapped me in warm blankets under the wagon. Slowly, the heat from the fire warmed me and I stopped shivering.

"Tell the rest, Bezellion," young Peter beckoned the trader.

Peter Bezellion finished. "I thought Hans would never rescue his son. The water was rising. The current was swifter. A tangled mass of logs and brush came bobbing toward Hans. Would it overtake him? But Hans's horse, Prince, knew his duty. His neck muscles tightened as he leaped into the treacherous waters. Peter was gone, but God directed Prince. Suddenly, Hans leaned to the side. I thought both he and the horse would capsize. Then they all disappeared!

"When they appeared again, there was a terrible struggle. Hans's arm grasped Prince's neck as he swung himself on the horse's back. With his free hand, he flung Peter's limp body across Prince.

"As Prince's feet touched solid ground, Hans grabbed the lead horse by the bridle. With one hand on King's bridle and the other supporting Peter, it looked like Hans would be pulled from his horse. But, with both of his legs pushing deeply into Prince's side, they guided the team from the swift current. As the wagon, pulled by six horses, clamored up over the steep bank, the mass of logs rushed by. They were safe. Thank God! I grabbed the dangling reins and tied them to a tree. It took time to untangle the mass of rope harnesses and horses and to set the wagon on its wheels. All the while, I watched Hans, gasping for breath himself, labor to get Peter to breathe.

"It was cold and rainy. Hans would need warmth. After a number of tries, our Indian friends produced a few wisps of smoke. They tried again. As a column of smoke ascended from the drenched wood, they stacked wood around the smoke to dry. Finally, the flames leaped from the pile of smoking wood.

"I prepared to take over, should Hans exhaust himself. He saw me there beside him, but he never offered me his place of duty until Peter's breathing was steady. Only then did he walk to the fire and claim the warm blankets and hot tea prepared for him.

"After we repaired the harnesses sufficiently, Peter mounted his horse in front of an empty wagon and proceeded toward home. As we forded the many swollen streams, Hans would say, 'Thank God.'

"Hans is at Martin Grafs, quite exhausted, but he will come later."

Grandfather reminded the crowd that it was time for the meeting to begin.

Susanna, Maria Huber, Bright Star, and Feronica Graf crowded together on their bench, facing their grandmothers. The grandmothers sang heartily. Their faith had been revived as they again witnessed God's protecting hand.

Christian Wenger preached on the brevity of life and the swift waters which can take believers the wrong way. He urged all to seek the current that leads to heaven.

Susanna thanked God for those who carefully guided her into the right way.

Chapter 20

Grandmother At A Hearing

Cabins for those who had renounced the world were increasing all over the Conestoga Valley. Everyone was disturbed.

When Marie Sauer left her husband to live a life of spiritual virginity, word spread everywhere throughout Penn's Woods. Her husband declared that he could not live alone in the wilderness without a wife. If she refused to come home, he and their son would return to Germantown. Christopher was angry with Beissel, but Beissel, as usual, remained calm. No longer would Christopher share his printing interests with Beissel.

A loud cry went out against quite a number who had left their marriage companions. Apparently Beissel had powers that even the court didn't have.

The constable asked Deacon Martin Graf to accompany him to summon Beissel to court on a king's warrant. It was England's law that such wicked deeds should be sorely punished.

As the constable and deacon entered the clearing, they saw Beissel carrying a pitcher of water into a cabin. Remembering how difficult it was in the past to find Beissel, the constable knew that this time he had him. When they went to the door and asked for Beissel, the brother bade them to come in. While the constable guarded the door, the deacon searched the small one-room cabin thoroughly to no avail.

"We saw him enter here bearing that pitcher on the table. Where is he?" the constable demanded.

The brother refused to answer. The constable and deacon looked around the outside walls for a way of escape, but there was none. Bewildered, they concluded that the rumors about Beissel going through doors and walls and being invisible were true. Some claimed him to be like Jesus, but the deacon stated his opinion well when he declared, "Beissel is a witch."

The men left the cabin and turned around at the edge of the clearing. Alas, they saw Beissel come out the cabin door and flee in the opposite direction into the forest.

"The spirits protected him that time, but I'm not convinced he is of God," the constable complained. "Beissel's doctrine doesn't line up with my Lutheran beliefs."

Then a rumor spread that Beissel was guilty of immoral conduct. God had blessed the solitary with a baby, but no one knew where the baby was living.

Later, Beissel and the Eicher girl were called to a hearing to determine if they were guilty. Beissel demanded witnesses, but there were none. When the judge dismissed them, Beissel reproved him sharply for taking them from their Sabbath meeting.

Six weeks prior to this, Beissel had appointed Johannes Landis as an elder. The Landises had lived a life of continence, as did all of Beissel's group at this time, and were proving their usefulness to Beissel quite well.

After Beissel's trial, Johannes accused his wife of spending too much time at Beissel's cabin. "You are my wedded wife," he reminded her. "I will not give you up. You must be subject to me and stay at home."

But Johannes's wife soon visited Beissel again. Johannes ordered the constable to bring her home by force. He was angry and returned to Beissel, acting as though he would kill him, but Beissel escaped.

During Beissel's next meeting, Johannes entered, singing a terrible song about coming to kill Beissel. His listeners shrank from him in fear. *Would he kill them all?*

Suddenly, Landis rushed towards Beissel, grabbed him by the throat, and dragged him to the door. He would have killed him, had not the men tied his hands behind his back and chased him home.

Grandfather was talking about all these happenings while Grandmother was making supper.

"Surely the authorities won't allow these things to continue," Grandmother insisted. "What will the end of this be?"

Susanna wondered also.

Later, while they were eating they heard the sound of horse hoofs, announcing someone's arrival.

"It's the constable!" Grandfather exclaimed from the doorway.

"The constable?" Grandmother was surprised. "Surely none of us did wrong."

Grandfather searched the circle of innocent faces around the table. After his greeting, the constable asked Grandmother to appear at the hearing the next day.

"What has my dear wife done?" Grandfather asked.

"Perhaps wagged her tongue too much," the constable suggested. "All the older women in Earl Township are to bear witness to Beissel's recent conduct."

"I know only what I've heard," Grandmother said, trying to defend herself.

"And all that you have told someone else," the constable reproved her sternly. "All who are summoned must appear," he added, and abruptly left.

"I've been guilty. We women talked," Grandmother admitted. "I hope we don't have to pay a fine."

"They aren't trying to get money. They want to find out if the reports are true," Grandfather assured her. "We must have some law and order around here. Tomorrow you and I will leave early so we can get there on time."

☦ ☦ ☦ ☦

The next morning the family sent Grandfather and Grandmother on their way. All day and through the following night, the Ulrichs tried to imagine what might be happening. When the grandparents returned, the teenagers gathered around to hear what had taken place.

"Did Grandmother have to talk?" Susanna asked.

"Yes, Grandmother was questioned," Grandfather replied. "Each of the women told what they had heard and from whom. After Grandmother had given that information to the judge, she turned toward Anna Eicher and Beissel and said: 'No matter what the outcome, I am sorry that I passed on the rumor.' She admitted that, as a Christian, she should have kept silent.

"All the rumors were traced back to one woman. The accused said that she had said it about another married woman, not Anna Eicher.

"The judge asked for Anna Eicher to be pardoned; however, the court levied her household goods enough to pay for the cost of the hearing."

"Why would they do that if she wasn't guilty?" Christopher asked.

"Yes, it does sound strange, but we have no right to accuse her further," Grandfather told his listeners. "The Scripture says, 'Be sure your sin will find you out.' On the other hand, it would be terrible to accuse someone of something which she had not done."

☩ ☩ ☩ ☩

On the next Sabbath, when Johannes Landis's wife appeared at Beissel's meeting, the celibate brethren bade her to return home to her husband.

"How long should I stay at home?" she asked.

"Until you are asked to come again," they replied.

Johannes still feared that his wife might leave him. When the next love feast was held, Johannes tied her to the bed post, even though she assured him that she would stay home. Later, Beissel offered Johannes reconciliation, but he refused it. Beissel was grieved that he had been the cause of Johannes's becoming evil.

"Marie Hildebrand says that she is tired of the commotion," Peter announced one day. "Yesterday she left confinement to marry Alexander Mack's son at Germantown."

Susanna's eyes opened wide. "Might my sister Catherine come home, too?"

"Beissel says the church has conformed too much to the spirit of the world. Maybe he should return to the desert again, into solitude," Peter added soberly.

"It is a serious thing for a shepherd to leave his flock," Grandfather said.

"Was Beissel dressed in Quaker garb today?" Christopher asked.

"Yes, he was," Grandfather replied. "Recently, Samuel and Israel insisted that Beissel was more like the Quaker pietists than the German Baptists or Mennonites, so he should dress like them. Beissel left the garb on, and all his followers will follow his example."

"Will his Mennonite followers change to Quaker garb?" Christopher asked.

"With all the immorality and witchcraft, they have more reasons to leave Beissel than deciding what type of clothes to wear," Grandfather replied.

"Hopefully, Beissel won't be asking us grandmothers to be a witness in any more hearings for awhile," Grandmother concluded.

Chapter 21

Land Of Milk And Honey

"How do I reward two seventeen-year-old girls?" Grandfather asked. "Since Anna has gone to the Wengers, Susanna and Maria have milked five cows, skimmed the milk, and churned the butter."

At first Grandmother's eyes sparkled the way they always did when she had a good idea; but then her face became very serious. Susanna could not guess why.

✣ ✣ ✣ ✣

"Susanna! Wake up!" Maria called as she shook her. "Hurry!" she urged. "Grandfather is frying bacon, eggs, and scrapple for breakfast. Christian promised to read to us about the land of milk and honey today."

Where am I? Susanna wondered. *Oh yes, yesterday Maria and I began our trip, which is Grandfather's reward to us. We are hauling wheat and butter to Philadelphia with Grandfather, Peter, and Christian Eby. Last night, when we stopped, the moon was full and the sky was clear, which made camping easier.*

Susanna moved her stiff legs and slid out from under the warm blanket which Grandmother had made from Fluff Ball's wool. *Yesterday we walked, but today we'll ride,* Susanna remembered, since the trail was becoming smoother. Not far from their wagon two Indians lay sleeping in a three-sided shelter.

"This is our second day," Maria chattered. "Yesterday, on Peters Road, we forded Pequea Creek, Indian Run, Spring Run, the west fork of Brandywine Creek, and Beaver Creek. Last night we slept beside the oldest mill in the Conestoga Valley. We'll wash our faces in the east fork of the Brandywine and then ford it. We are on the Great Minquas Path, and tonight we'll sleep at William Penn's church."

"We've crawled through our grike and we're taking a trip!" Susanna recalled. "I dreamed of this trip as I printed 'S' for Shakamaxon on the blocks of butter. There William Penn made a treaty with the Indians. I'd like to stand at the spot where it was done."

"I dreamed of this trip as I printed 'P' for Philadelphia on the blocks of butter," Maria laughed. "That reminded me to work our butter carefully."

"It took a long time to clean the wheat good enough to pass Grandmother's inspection," Susanna remembered. "Then we stored it in the loft. The bitter taste of rye grass spread under the baskets kept the squirrels away."

"Grandfather hopes to get $100 for the wheat so he can pay our taxes," Maria remembered. "The rest will go for things which we need."

"What is in the barrel on the back of our wagon?" Susanna whispered.

"Hush! Peter told us not to ask that question until we return home. We must not talk about that barrel to anyone," Maria reminded her.

Steam curled out of a birch bark knapsack in the fire. The flames did not burn it because it was filled with water for tea. The thought of hot tea made Susanna feel warm all over.

Then Susanna saw an extra bowl of food. Something told her that maybe the man who lived where the water flows upstream was in that barrel. Next, the dish was gone! *I'll likely never see that man. Yet he is so near*, she thought wistfully.

As the wagon began rumbling along, Susanna figured its contents aloud: "The six crocks hold 200 pounds of butter; the rest of the wagon is full of bags of wheat, feed for the oxen, and the grease bucket."

"And straw to sit on, ten dozen eggs, our clothes, and lunch," Maria added. "Is Christian Eby going to Germantown for a special reason?" she asked.

"Yes. On his trip to Europe to fetch his brother, he met a girl who interested him," Grandfather replied. "She is at sea with her parents. Some fishermen saw their ship a week ago. We'll go to the dock first to see if they've arrived. Some of the other Mennonites who are with them will return with us to the Conestoga Valley."

Christian invited the girls to sit on his wagon while he read Falckner's *Trip to Pennsylvania*. Falckner listed more than thirty items Europeans were to bring with them to Pennsylvania.

"My father was too poor to bring all of those things," Christian commented. "He writes about a bothersome frog. It is very large and emits such abominable bellowing at night that he sounds like a young bull."

"I like to hear grandfather frogs," Maria challenged Falckner's idea.

"Falckner exaggerates too much," Peter said after Christian had read more.

"Wait 'til you hear this!" Christian pulled a letter from his bag. "Sauer sent this letter to his friends in Germany in 1725— seven years ago. He found Penn's Woods flowing with milk and honey. Apple trees had so much fruit that much of it spoiled because there weren't enough people to pick it. He called this place an earthly paradise. One could buy land that would yield large profits of gold and silver."

"Sauer doesn't know that a few years before his arrival, our harvest was very small. Everyone went hungry," Peter interrupted.

Christian went on, "He writes about religious freedom. . . ."

"Religious freedom! So much that his wife leaves the religion he has for another man's religion," Peter said with disgust. "Freedom, indeed, to leave one's loved ones. Marie isn't making any move to go back with him. What kind of letters does Sauer write now?"

"Not that kind, I'm sure," Christian exclaimed. "But you must admit that God has blessed us with religious freedom like our people have never known."

"Yes, I thank God every day for our freedom," Peter replied soberly.

"Why is there a big circle of burnt trees about us?" Maria asked later.

"Some wagons carrying hemp caught fire from brush that was burning along the road. The hemp burned so violently that it destroyed everything around it," Peter replied.

In the evening the group left the forest and began to see cabins. This was Marion. Nearby was the church where William Penn's family worshipped. It was ten miles further to the Schuylkill River. Darkness came, and they stopped. Grandfather's warm fire gave them light. The roasted rabbit and johnny cakes tasted good. Christian greased the wagons while Peter cared for the oxen. They were weary and slept well. Tomorrow would be another long day of travel.

✢ ✢ ✢ ✢

"Get up!" Maria summoned and Susanna awoke. "After we cross the Schuylkill River, it's only a mile to Philadelphia and the Delaware River."

It was dawn when they arrived at the Schuylkill. "This river is wider than even the schwamm," Susanna exclaimed. The wide river bed was lined with forest on both sides. As they forded the river, the water became deeper. The wagon wheels left the river's floor, and they floated.

Susanna was leery. The experience Peter Graf had when he almost drowned in the Brandywine Creek was still fresh on her mind. If the wagon upset, she guessed she would hang on to it.

"The river is lower than usual. Though the water is deep, it isn't very wide," Grandfather said matter-of-factly. "Hans Graf's horses are trained to go through much deeper water than this."

Susanna forgot her fear. The river's waters rocked the wagon gently as the fresh, cool breeze greeted her face. It was invigorating. Too soon their wagons reached the shallow water and were rattling down the cobblestone street of Philadelphia. They passed dull-looking rows of what Peter called brick houses and saw more new things than her eyes had ever seen.

"This is Philadelphia, the City of Brotherly Love," Peter announced. "See the glass windows that came from England," he added. "When you look through them, things appear awkward and out of proportion."

As they passed William Penn's fine buildings, they saw the wharf through the trees. A ship at the dock rocked gently with the incoming waves. Further down the river, Susanna imagined that she saw the river emptying into the ocean. Stopping, Christian gained permission to go aboard. Susanna waited eagerly to see this lady.

"The ship that we came on wasn't as nice as this one," Grandfather remarked. "Still, I never wish to be swayed on the ocean again."

Christian returned alone. "They arrived last night and were taken to Germantown this morning. There are people on the boat still waiting to become redemptioners," he said sadly.

Next, the group went to the warehouse where Peter and Christian unloaded the wagons. The mysterious barrel was pulled further toward the front with some other barrels that Grandfather had purchased. When a sneeze erupted from the barrel, the girls looked questioningly at Peter. Peter looked straight ahead.

As soon as Grandfather and Christian returned with their heavy bags of silver dollars, they hurried to the tax collector to pay their taxes.

By now the town was full of fashionably dressed English people who rushed through the streets in fine carriages. With their manes flying and loud snorting, the horses pranced valiantly by. The horses' hooves tapped loudly down the dirty cobblestone street.

When the coachman used his whip, the echo of its sharp crack traveled through the treetops. When he said, "Whoa," the horses obediently stood still with their heads cocked like statues. Impatiently, their nostrils blew in and out in disagreement, and their flanks heaved heavily.

"If those wagons don't slow down, they will crash," Maria insisted.

Grandfather was eager to go. He wanted to follow the Delaware River northward before going west to Germantown. Also, tomorrow was Sunday and Peter mischievously decided that Christian Eby had better make it to the Germantown Meetinghouse by morning.

"I never knew wagons could go so fast on such smooth roads," Susanna cried out. She grasped her bonnet and shawl to keep them from blowing away.

"If we had springs in our wagons, we'd ride like queens," Maria giggled.

"So, you wish to dress proudly and drive in fancy wagons!" Peter teased.

"Never. Those teamsters claim the whole road," Maria sighed wearily. "I'm tired of Philadelphia's dirty, smelly streets."

"You girls did an excellent job of salting down the butter," Grandfather praised them. "The wheat sold for top price because you cleaned it well. You may buy woolen stockings as part of your reward."

"Oh, bought stockings fit so nicely!" Susanna thanked Grandfather heartily. "Truly, we live in a land of milk and honey!"

Chapter 22

Germantown

The place was beautiful! A ship from England sailed leisurely beside them as they followed the wide Delaware River northward. Tired, sick-looking people were lined on the deck. Susanna understood the sea stories those folks would have to tell.

"Susanna and Peter, your family and mine came down this road from New York many years ago," Grandfather informed them. "The road is smoother, but things looked the same. Your parents were ill, and it was one of the most pleasant moments in their last days of suffering."

"I'm glad we can be together to enjoy this like our parents did," Peter said with feeling. "I was only a few years old and don't remember."

Susanna breathed in the fresh breeze from the river. "This probably seemed like heaven to our parents," she imagined aloud.

"It was. Your father said that if heaven could be better, he could hardly fathom it. Your mother was so frail and tired, she just sat silently and enjoyed it," Grandfather recalled.

Christian stopped the wagons near the largest elm tree that Susanna had ever seen. "Many years ago, under this tree, Penn made the only treaty with the Indians that has never been broken," Christian told them. "This elm is not high, but I'd say it has a twenty-four-foot spread. The name of this place is Shakamaxon."

The girls hurriedly led the way toward that important place, and the rest followed behind with their lunch.

"Thank God, we have a land of freedom," Grandfather said respectfully. "We ate our lunch here, also, when we first arrived."

For the next three hours the group traveled on rough road through the forest. After awhile, Grandfather called, "We'll sleep here at Deacon Abraham Reiff's for the night." It was dark.

Susanna remembered nothing except that she crawled into a tick and slept. Familiar breakfast aromas awoke her. "Maria, we are in Germantown," she announced. They shook their ticks and went down the ladder to the fireplace.

"Welcome to Germantown! Did you sleep well?" Mrs. Reiff wondered.

"Very well," both girls answered gratefully.

"This is Elizabeth Moyer," she said, introducing the young lady standing nearby.

"You came with Christian Eby," Elizabeth spoke knowingly. "You are Maria Huber and Susanna Ulrich. Abraham's wife told me about you. Tomorrow my family and I will travel with you to the Conestoga Valley. I was ready to waken you so we can go to the meeting at Germantown. It's new and interesting in America!" She sounded unusually happy.

Susanna was enthused with Elizabeth's joy. *Hmm. She would make a good wife for someone.*

Soon the group was on its way to the Germantown Meetinghouse. The Hubers, Ulrichs, Reiffs, Christian Eby, and Elizabeth Moyer traveled together. They passed many plainly dressed Quakers going to their church. "Their meetinghouse is where your sister Catherine went to school," Maria reminded them.

"Hans and Peter Graf are here, too," Grandfather told them. "Barbara Horst and her sons arrived recently and will be traveling home with the Grafs and us. The Horsts' trunks were left behind so the captain could accommodate more passengers on board. That meant their clean clothes, food, and money were gone. Then, her husband died at sea. Her boys will work for Hans Graf until their way is paid. Joseph is nine."

"That sounds different than Falckner's trip to America," Susanna concluded.

At the meetinghouse they met the Hockman and Klemmer families who had just arrived. There were backless benches, and the Reiffs showed them where to sit. Susanna marveled at the singing in the big room filled with so many people.

After two long messages, what she had expected happened. Bishop Rittenhouse asked Christian Eby and Elizabeth Moyer to come forward, and he married them. Susanna sat in solemn suspense as she saw and heard it all. The couple planned to settle at Hammer Creek, Lancaster County.

When the travelers were ready to leave, Grandfather talked with Christopher Dock, who was visiting Germantown. Susanna and

Maria listened as he told them about his school in Skippack. Susanna had never dreamed that she would meet the teacher whom the people back home admired so much. "Maybe someday we can go to a school like this," she suggested to Maria.

"Maybe some day," Maria managed hopefully, "but we'll soon be too old."

The next day Grandfather, Susanna, and Maria walked down Germantown's only street. At the woolen mill along the Wissahickon Creek, her grandfather bought what Maria called their "precious woolen stockings."

While at the mill, Grandfather talked with some young Amish men. "They were Widow Yoder's boys," he explained later. "They say that more Amish want to come when they find a way."

After stopping at the tannery for leather to make boots, the wagons started for the Conestoga Valley. Grandfather took the women, girls, and Joseph Horst in his wagon. The two barrels remained at the back. The men found room on top of the other wagons, which were filled with their possessions. It was a joyous group on the last lap of the new arrivals' journey in a land of religious freedom.

"That was our dream come true. We've been to Germantown," Susanna shared with Maria.

Susanna turned cold. "What if he discovers the contents of the mysterious barrels?"

Chapter 23

City Of Brotherly Love

The group passed noisy mills of all kinds along the Wissahickon Creek in Germantown. Where the Wissahickon emptied into the Schuylkill River, Christian stopped at Rittenhouse's paper mill to buy some paper, which was still hard to find. Susanna and Maria stood on the footbridge that went over the mill race while Grandfather talked with Bishop Rittenhouse.

As the travelers followed the Schuylkill River south toward Philadelphia, they saw large clouds of smoke in the sky ahead of them. In Philadelphia, they found a group of houses burning. Grandfather said that many houses burned there as a result of chimney fires.

After stopping at the Trader's Shop where Hans Graf traded his furs, Grandfather told them about the slave block ahead. They saw a child cruelly taken from his mother and sold as the mother wept and the child screamed. Other black families were crying and embracing as they waited to be sold and separated forever. One of the fathers started fighting and was brutally whipped.

Beside the block, Susanna saw an Irishman bidding for slaves. Then she remembered! He was the man who had called Theodorus Eby a dumb Dutchman. She turned cold. *What if he discovers the contents of the mysterious barrels?* But, really, she did not know what—or who—was in those two barrels.

"There is wickedness, no matter where we go," Grandfather spoke sadly after they had passed. All were silent, left with their own thoughts.

When they stopped for lunch on the other side of the Schuylkill, Christian Eby challenged Hans Graf. "How can you call such a wicked place an elysian dale? Is this place like heaven?"

Susanna listened closely. What would he say?

"If we see the good in life and allow God to take care of the rest, even a most unlovely place can be like heaven," Hans explained.

"How could William Penn call Philadelphia the City of Brotherly Love when he bought slaves at the auction stand?" Christian prodded further.

"True, he did," Hans agreed, "but his conscience must have pricked him in the end. He freed all of his slaves in his will."

Susanna pondered Hans's answer as they started traveling again.

"Look out ahead!" Peter exclaimed. A string of twelve horses came toward them. One man rode on the first and another man took the rear. The horses in between were heavily loaded with packs.

"They are French traders coming from Ohio and Illinois," Peter Ulrich explained. "Each horse probably carries about 200 pounds of goods. Looks like they are carrying furs." He knew that Hans and Peter Graf traveled like that when the trails were bad.

At dusk the group stopped to camp for the night. While they were eating around the campfire, they noticed another group nearby also preparing to camp for the night.

As the girls were making a bed for the women and themselves under the wagon, they saw Peter and an unfamiliar woman standing beside them.

"Take this lady into your bed to sleep between you. Go to sleep immediately," Peter instructed. "During the night I will come for the three of you. You must follow me as we travel on foot. Don't make a sound. Even the snapping of a twig could mean immediate trouble."

Susanna and Maria followed his bidding. For a moment, the light from the fireplace allowed them to see the woman's face. What she saw told Susanna what was happening.

The three of them could not sleep, but they lay very still. Susanna remembered Grandmother's sober face. *Grandmother knew about this and is surely awake and praying for us*, she consoled herself.

Before long, Peter was leaning over them, bidding them to come. Quietly they followed him into the forest where they met Peter Graf and another man. The man and woman clasped hands and followed Peter Graf. Maria, Susanna, and Peter moved speedily behind them. How grateful Susanna was for Bright Star's lessons on how to run noiselessly. Peter Graf knew the shortcuts that crossed the winding trail. After they had crossed the trail, they heard horses' hooves.

"Hide!" Peter Graf whispered.

From behind a large tree Susanna could hear the rider come closer, and then passing them. When he was out of hearing range, Peter whispered to the man, "That was your master!"

"I know," the black man answered. "What will we do now?"

"Stay here in silence and pray," Peter answered calmly. "He must have guessed that we would leave camp, and he is looking for us. He'll be back for the slaves by morning because his helper can't move them alone."

It seemed like they were waiting for a long time. Susanna's teeth chattered from the cold. She thought about her own soul. Should she confess her sinful state and forsake sin to follow the Lord? Yet, she wasn't sure that now was the time. She was afraid. Where did they find this woman? What was the story?

After a long time, they heard the slow trot of horses' hooves coming back. "Don't look. Stay hidden. He is looking," Peter whispered. "Run for your life if he sees us."

Susanna held her breath as the horse went by, then stopped. Was the rider looking for tracks on the trail? He jumped from his horse. Twigs snapped as he walked around. Then, mounting his horse, he moved slowly toward camp.

When the man was gone, Peter urged the others toward home. Their feet were wet from fording the creeks. At daybreak, they passed the Paxton Trail, which went toward the iron works. After another mile, they stopped to wait for the wagon. Finally, Susanna, Maria, and their friend, Jemima, made a bed for themselves in the leaves. Jemima told them how they had brought her husband to get her. Her master had gladly set her free and sent her to the Conestoga Valley with her husband. But, still, her husband's master refused to free him, even with the offers of large sums. Sleep didn't come, but they rested until they heard the wagons coming.

No sooner had they started walking when they heard horses' hooves behind them. Again Joel and Jemima jumped into the barrels. As the rider behind them drew nearer, they moved on. Susanna didn't realize how tired she was. Her only desire was to get home to Grandmother.

The horse which was close behind Maria and her stopped. Susanna was terrified. The Irishman always carried a gun. For a moment she saw the man's angry face as he shook his fist at them.

Looking straight ahead, she walked fast, praying earnestly that God would spare them.

Next, Hans Graf and Christian Eby rode back past them toward the Irishman. Susanna looked back and saw the three of them talking. The Irishman held his fist in front of Hans's face.

Peter Graf passed them, his face pale, as he traveled back to his father.

Susanna and Maria walked and prayed until they heard riders behind them again. This time it was Hans, Christian, and Peter, their faces beaming with joy.

"You are a free man. We paid plenty for your freedom," Hans announced as he and Christian climbed from their horses into the wagon. "Hopefully, your master has shaken his fist at you for the last time."

Everyone stopped to see what was happening.

Joel and Jemima were out of their barrels in an instant. "Thank you, thank you!" Joel cried as he threw his arms about Hans and Christian. "Somehow, I hope to return that money to you."

"We are both free, thank God!" Jemima exclaimed as she cried with the girls.

Already Grandfather was building a fire. "When the Irishman made trouble this morning, we left without breakfast," he explained. "Now we shall eat."

Suddenly, Susanna realized how hungry she was, but that didn't matter. Joel and Jemima were both free.

Conestoga Valley isn't a city, but surely it will be a place of brotherly love to Joel and Jemima, Susanna decided to herself.

CHAPTER 24

Magdelena's Lookout

The Christian Wenger family needed help, and Grandfather's cabin was full. Grandfather and the three Ulrichs decided that the Ulrichs should stay at the Wengers for awhile. They would return and help Grandfather as needed. Susanna was helping Magdelena for a few weeks.

"Where did you learn about herbs?" Susanna asked, as she helped Magdelena in her garden.

Every corner of Magdelena's herb garden was filled with clumps of young shoots. There were thorstem, hops, and rotolofa with leaves shaped like a geranium. Magdelena knew which part of each plant to use for healing. Some were used in tea, poultices, or ointment. They were preserved in alcohol or oil, or they were dried.

"I studied the use of herbs in Switzerland while Hans was in military training," Magdelena answered. "Later, as I searched for Hans in the Palatinate and then in Holland, I used the knowledge which I had learned.

"There was much sickness among our Anabaptist people. Many were injured from gruesome tortures. I comforted them and eased their suffering. Often, I thanked God for sparing Hans from the sin of persecuting the Anabaptists."

"And you are still soothing men's hurts," Susanna praised her respectfully. "The way you, Hans, and Anna live has impressed us. You are serving others unselfishly. Anna's children are trained to be useful. Hans assists the Indians by trading blankets for hides. He pays many people's passage to America and helps them find land."

"Yes, and he paid Anna's passage, too," Magdelena recalled. "She was left sick and alone on the ship, wondering what would happen to her. Since I was supposedly dead, Hans had mercy on Anna, paid her way, and then married her."

"Aren't you lonely up here sometimes?" Susanna wondered.

"Yes," Magdelena replied. "It is lonely to live alone. I'm grateful for the times when you girls come to stay with me. Conestoga Valley's rugged trails can be discouraging. From my lookout, I remember the many needy faces down there, and my problems seem small. Conestoga Valley holds many heart-breaking troubles because of selfishness.

"Submission to God and the church is hard for selfish people. He who gives himself up finds submission easy. Let's go up to the lookout," Magdelena suggested.

They climbed up around the cliff to the cabin. Magdelena stopped for her spy glass, and they continued up the steep hill to the top. "This is like climbing a cat's back," Magdelena puffed. "We call the Indian path over the top Katze Boucle Path."

The wood-clad hills and valleys were enchanting. Susanna's people lived down there in the trees. Earlier, when the oak leaves were the size of a squirrel's ears, she had planted corn. Today, the oak leaves were larger, and the view was breathtaking.

"There are trees everywhere!" Susanna exclaimed when they reached the clearing at the top. From the slate trail they saw the wigwams of Magdelena's Indian friends. Not far from them was the Conestoga Creek. The lake of green foliage breathed back and forth with the breeze like a sea of water. "Don't you ever get lost in this wilderness?" Susanna asked.

"When a needy person asks God to show him the way, God is faithful," Magdelena replied soberly. "Peter Graf marked every trail on a map for me. Hans gave me Lady, his best horse. She is easy to ride and knows the trails. When I need help, I set Lady loose and she goes to Anna's cabin or the nearest neighbor. Help soon arrives."

"Look at the two close columns of smoke," Magdelena pointed directly south. "People are kindling their fires for supper. The column to the left is Anna Graf's; the other one is the Wengers'. Do you like living with them?"

"Yes, I like it. I miss Grandfather and Grandmother, but the Wengers need help," Susanna replied. "The Eberlys are helping Grandfather and Grandmother, so my brothers and I moved to the Wengers."

"Eve has plenty of work. She needs you," Magdelena emphasized.

"The haze of smoke at the right of the Wengers is the Nageles' home and the cabins of the brotherhood. In the distance beyond that, at the foot of the mountains, is the Strasburg settlement. To the right, where the mountains end, are the Pequea settlements."

Susanna's imagination followed the places that lay under the mass of leaves.

"Beyond the far end of this cat's back, the Cocalico Creek flows into the Conestoga Creek. Northwest, at the Long's barn at Mill Way, the Hammer Creek and Middle Creek empty into the Cocalico.

"At the left end of this mountain closest to us is Emanuel Eckerlin's cabin. The column of smoke rises as he washes down his acorn bread with acorn coffee." Magdelena's smile chased the wrinkles from her face as she spoke. "Beyond him, near the distant mountain, is Indiantown where Quick Foot's brothers live."

Susanna directed the spy glass toward Indiantown. "Where did you get this spy glass?" she asked Magdelena, her hand touching the long wooden tube.

"A sea captain, who is a friend of Hans, gave it to me," Magdelena answered. Her hand moved from Indiantown to a point directly east of them. In the distance the mountains looked like chimneys. "No one lives in that area. Between the chimneys and us is Weber Thal."

"Between that ridge and the Welsh Mountain is Grandfather's house," Susanna exclaimed. "I've never seen it from up here."

"The smoke to the right of your home is from the convent and Quick Foot's cabin. One cabin near there is empty," Magdelena commented sadly. "Christopher Sauer has returned to Germantown. He says that this wilderness is no place to raise a son without a mother. His son will attend Germantown School next winter. Now he helps his father in the shop."

"What kind of shop does he have?" Susanna questioned. Her mind went to Germantown and the busy street she saw last fall.

"The sign on his door says, 'Christopher Sauer, clockmaker.' He sells books and medicines, and is also a wheelwright and optician. I buy medicine there," Magdelena informed her.

They watched the sun sink behind the mountain in the west. The ridges were fringed with gold. Rays of soft mellow light floated on the endless mass of leaves. The sound of cowbells from below reminded Susanna that they weren't alone. A call, "*Soolk, soolk,*" came from the direction of Anna Graf's.

"Grafs' cows must have wandered away today," Magdelena figured. Next the joyous song of Anna's daughter rang through the valley below. Her song was harmonious to the hour. She finally directed the cows toward another insistent cry of "*Soolk, soolk.*"

Susanna thought about her happy days at Grandfather's house and now at the Wengers' home. She thought about her brothers and Gabriel Eckerlin and their many talks with Christian and Eve Wenger around the fireplace. In each of these homes, all were considerate of each other. Children honored their elders; happiness reigned.

Susanna knew that Aunt Anna would enjoy teaching the Eberlys and Jacob's children next winter. Already Jacob Huber was making benches and tables for their classroom.

"Do you see the column of smoke coming from the top of Welsh Mountain?" Magdelena interrupted her thoughts. "I found that place from where the water flows upstream. Joel and Jemima have a little boy. The Ebys often go up there to help them read the Bible."

Through the spy glass, Susanna tried to see the stream that ran uphill, but its strange waters were hidden beneath the foliage and evergreens. "Does the water really flow upstream?" Susanna was still suspicious.

"Depending where you stand, it seems to flow upstream," Magdelena smiled. "We all know that water doesn't really run uphill."

"A spy glass is like the Bible. It shows us the way. If ever you need help and encouragement, come here and rest awhile. Read my Bible and let God take hold of your life," Magdelena encouraged her. "I am one of your adopted grandmothers who prays for every orphan in the Conestoga Valley."

Susanna smiled warmly at her kind friend, but then she looked down. *Maybe I can tell Magdelena how I feel. Magdelena is kind and understanding.*

"Is something troubling you, Susanna? Would you like to talk about it?" Magdelena asked with a tenderness that few women possessed.

"Yes, I feel so wicked and guilty lately," Susanna managed to say.

"Have you done wrong things that need to be made right?" Magdelena wondered.

"Some. I want to do right, but something in me wants to do wrong."

"You need to come to the Lord. It says in I John 1:9, 'If we confess our sins, He is faithful and just to forgive us our sins and to cleanse us from all unrighteousness.' You need to repent of your sins, Susanna," Magdelena explained simply. "That's what I did, and my life has been changed."

At Magdelena's suggestion, Susanna readily knelt by a rock beside Magdelena and prayed. She confessed her sin and discovered the peace which God gives to those who repent of their sins. She promised to make restitution where it was needed.

"God bless you and keep you, Susanna," Magdelena said with joy. "Your battleground with Satan will now begin. He may come as an angel of light, or he may bring clouds of despair in your life; but God makes a way of escape. When you have peace with God, you discover that bit of heaven within."

The soft, balmy air and last rays of mellow sunset were lovelier than before. "Thank you, Magdelena, for sharing your lookout and helping me find peace. I have joy like I've never known!" Susanna exclaimed happily.

CHAPTER 25

A Dream Come True

Because of the false doctrine afloat, the leaders decided that school was a must for their children. On the first day of school, the students were seated around the table at the Wenger home. Joseph Horst was in the lower class. He would be learning from the *ABC Book* by J. P. Schabalies, which lay in front of him.

The middle class sat at the other end of the table. They could already read, so they would be learning more difficult lessons. There were six in the middle class: Hans Graf's children—Hannah, Mary, John, David, and Feronica—and also Susanna Ulrich.

Susanna was rejoicing. "I am seventeen and this is my first year in a real school." She was thankful that Grandfather and Grandmother had taught her to read.

The upper class would attend only in the morning. There were six young men: Gabriel Eckerlin; Christopher and Peter Ulrich; and Samuel, Marx, and Peter Graf.

Again, Susanna counted the thirteen ink wells in the center of the table. She made ink by boiling crushed walnut shells in water and adding vinegar to make the ink set. Each softstone well also contained a crow quill which Christopher had mercilessly pulled from an unwelcome crow at the cratch. After each student had perfectly written his assignment by memory, he would copy it, using ink on his prized paper.

Three *Ausbunds* (hymn books), three prayer books, *The Works of Menno Simons*, *The Wandering Soul*, and *The Dortrecht Confession of Faith* were stacked on a shelf on the wall. A large Bible laid open at the end of the table. Beside the wall calendar hung the map which Grandfather had gotten from the shipmaster.

Susanna's dreaming ended when Christian Wenger called the school to order. After a song, Bible reading, and prayer, classes began.

Brother Christian addressed the middle class. "You may write the numbers from one to ten on your slates, and also the upper and lower case of the alphabet. As you finish, bring your work to me. Sometime today, please copy Psalm 1 on your slate and memorize it as soon as possible.

"The upper class may read pages one to four of the first chapter of *The Wandering Soul*. I will test you with questions by ten o'clock."

There was a scratching of soapstones on slates as they began. Joseph started learning his ABCs and writing them as Brother Christian required. Susanna struggled to write her letters perfectly. She was still memorizing when they were told to copy math problems from the slate on the wall.

Before lunch, the upper class answered Brother Christian's questions and took turns reading aloud from the prayer book, followed by singing a difficult song from the *Ausbund*. Their class assignment for the month was to copy Grandfather's map on a large piece of paper; however, this could not be done during class.

While they ate their lunch, one of the students from the upper class read from the Old Testament.

"How big is America?" Joseph Horst asked after lunch.

Pointing to Hans Huber's map, Brother Christian used a stick to follow the heavy black line around the land which sailors thought to be America. "This is America," he explained. "It would take many months to travel across it."

"Were we the first people here?" Joseph asked again.

"Indians were here a long time before the white man arrived," Brother Christian answered. "European ships traveled a long way around Africa to get to the East Indies. In 1492, two hundred years before our people came, Columbus was looking for a shortcut to the East Indies. He found a small island off the American coast. The coconut palm trees and beautiful shells on its coral reefs didn't interest him. On the map a Spanish flag and a palm tree are drawn beside his boat.

"In 1513, Ponce de Leon, a Catholic from Spain, came looking for gold. He established a settlement in Florida, but the Indians did not trust Catholics who carried guns. On the map there is a Spanish flag waving from their fort.

"At that time, our people wanted to bring the gospel to the American Indians." Christian told them. "God was keeping Penn's Woods for us, but He wanted us to spread the gospel in Europe first.

Persecution from the Swiss leaders scattered our people and spread the gospel everywhere.

"In 1534, Cartier of France sailed up the Hudson River to find the East Indies. He found rapids, fish, furs, and five large lakes. The French flag reminds us of their presence until this day."

"Peter Bezellion is a French trader," Mary Graf added. "My father meets French traders when he trades with Indians along the Susquehanna."

"In 1607, England founded the Jamestown Colony in Virginia," Christian said, as he pointed to the slave blocks on the map. "The Indians feared the English who sold stolen Negroes and made them into slaves."

"God's hand has guided us here," Brother Christian exclaimed with joy. "Those seeking the East Indies and its gold have found only furs, fish, fighting Indians, and frustrations. God doesn't promise eternal reward to men who seek treasures for themselves. We'll gladly exchange hardship for freedom as we develop the land for you and your children.

"Because of persecution from the Church of England, the Pilgrims came to Massachusetts in 1620. When two Quakers came by, they hung one and chased away the other. The gallows drawn beside the fort reminds us that one who receives freedom can thoughtlessly take it from others.

"At about the same time, the Congregationalists who settled near the Pilgrims refused to allow a ship with Baptists to land on shore. The Baptists settled further south in Rhode Island.

"In 1634, Maryland was given to Catholics who also didn't have the freedom they desired in England."

I hope Maryland Catholics will be more tolerant than the Catholics who persecuted our fathers in Europe, Susanna decided.

>*Susanna remembered Grandfather's lessons. Only fifty years before, William Penn, a Quaker, was given Penn's Woods by King Charles II of England. Penn brought 200 persons with him and established Philadelphia, the City of Brotherly Love. He invited the Anabaptists and anyone who was willing to live under his holy experiment to come. All races, nationalities, and religions could live their own way, each respecting their different neighbors.*

In 1685, Pastorius brought the first Mennonite Germans to Germantown. The German Baptists had arrived two years earlier. By 1690, more German Mennonites arrived. Some moved to Skippack where Jacob Rittenhouse built the first paper mill in America. Susanna recalled shaking hands with him.

Four years later, the first Mennonite Swiss Brethren, led by Hans Graf, arrived in Germantown. Susanna counted it a privilege to live in the only colony in the New World that didn't have a church-and-state government. Yet, in spite of freedom, the Scotch and Irish people still greedily squatted on Indian territory, hoping to take their land by force. Then they wanted the Mennonites to help them fight the angry Indians.

Too soon the first day of school was over. Susanna milked the cows and fed the animals. She wondered how Aunt Anna's school, with twenty-seven pupils, went today.

Later, Gabriel split wood as Susanna carried it to the fireplace. "Did you like school today?" he asked.

"Yes. What I've dreamed of all my life has come true," she replied happily.

"It was like a dream come true for me, too," Gabriel returned. "Christian knows many things. He is a man of strong Christian character. I'm glad you've decided to follow the Lord, Susanna. Christian's teaching will be a help to both of us."

Gabriel carried the heaviest logs in for her. It was here at the wood pile that they had talked about many things. He was like a brother to her.

Chapter 26

Worse Than A Locust Plague

"Locusts are swarming everywhere!" Susanna cried. "They've stripped the trees, garden, and orchard, and they stain the laundry as it dries on the fence. One even sat on the table this morning. At least there is enough grass for the cows."

"The animals in the forest are thin, because the locusts eat their food," Maria added. "Our meat will be lean this year. Hopefully, the locusts will leave before the summer is over."

"Eve says there is less work since the locusts have devoured our food," Susanna laughed. "Maybe we'll spend more time reading our Bible and praying, since there is no food to put away. Christian suggested that we could eat locusts like John the Baptist."

"The German Baptists haven't had meetings since last February," Maria said. "At least Beissel called his congregation together, ordained elders, and gave them a Bible to use as their guide before he left. They are too confused and argumentative to meet together anymore."

"Beissel said he never expected the church to succeed, and that he was going to enter the solitary life in Emanuel's cabin. He went back there, cleared some land, and planted a garden. He's having a hard time getting rid of the evil spirits in that den of serpents. His garden was probably eaten by the locusts, too," Susanna added.

"The brethren at the convent didn't want to be German Baptists, so Samuel and a few others built another cabin near Emanuel's. Emanuel gave his cabin to Beissel and moved in with the brothers from the convent. They call themselves Fathers of the Desert.

"Beissel has given them new names. Emanuel is Elimelech; Samuel is Jekhume; Israel is Onesimus; and Beissel is Brother Friedsam Gottrecht.

"The women at the Sisters' Convent don't know what to do without Beissel either," Maria talked on. "Last week the Eicher girls asked Beissel if they could move there, too. The Fathers in the Desert do not want anything to do with the Eicher girls, and refused to allow them to come. But, by the end of the week, Beissel convinced them that it was of the Lord. Reluctantly, they agreed to build a cabin on the other side of the creek for the Eicher girls. They'll probably not be in a hurry to do it. The German Baptists have spread the news all over Penn's Woods. As people hear about it, they cry, 'Seduction!'"

"No!" Susanna exclaimed. "They are giving themselves a terrible name."

"Father knows the Hesses, Bombergers, and Oberholtzers who live west of Mill Way. He would like to move up there away from this fuss," Maria informed Susanna.

"Were you surprised when Marx Graf and Aunt Anna were married?" Susanna asked.

"No, I saw our deacon come to visit Grandfather and Anna in the spring," Maria smiled. "When Marx built his shop, I figured that he was ready to go on his own and would need a wife. They always did fit together except when Aunt Anna wanted to go into solitude. She acted different then."

"I wasn't surprised when Peter Graf married Susanna Musselman either," Susanna added. "He had their cabin finished, but his mill will not be running because the locusts ate the grain crops. It's full of people and troubles there, so he wants to go west."

"That would be better than seeing your partner go with Beissel and your joys of life being eaten away," Maria figured. "Did Christian buy one of Ben Franklin's German newspapers?"

"No. And they sold so poorly that Franklin didn't print more than two issues. Hans Graf bought one. Eve wishes the locusts would leave as fast as the printing of that newspaper. Everyone knows that Samuel and Beissel put Ben Franklin up to publishing it. The papers may not have been safe to read anyway."

"It's good we came to the meeting early so we have a chance to talk," Maria decided. "Who is that coming with the Carpenter boys?"

"It's Hans Zimmerman. He's fifteen years old and arrived without his family last week on the *Pink Plaisance*. The Carpenters are his relatives," Susanna said.

"Samuel is building a mill and asking for donations of grain to feed the poor," Maria continued. "Grandfather is giving his extra grain to our people at Weber Thal. Their area was hit the worst."

"Have you seen Catherine lately?" Susanna asked.

"Mother found her in the schwamm picking greens last fall," Maria replied. "Since she had pneumonia, her cough is worse. She is weak and terribly thin. Father is almost ready to bring her home."

"I wish he would," Susanna almost shouted. "Can't all of Marie's medicines and herbs make her well? The locusts ate much of the food that Catherine was eating."

"Jacob Eberly is teaching our school this fall so that he can teach his brothers and sisters if necessary. He is urging his mother to leave Beissel and settle near Christian Eby's home on Hammer Creek," Maria told Susanna.

"Veronica looks discouraged. Her children aren't where she intended them to be; and now Beissel has left the sisters to themselves, also. She acts as if something worse than a locust plague has eaten at her. Someone needs to get both her and Catherine out of that place," Maria declared.

"Maybe they will come home now that Beissel has gone," Susanna suggested.

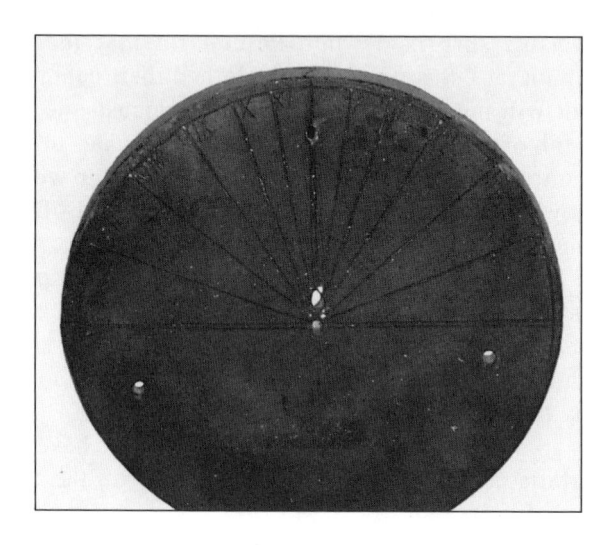

This clay sundial—actually a lid to a crock—was owned by Deacon Daniel Burkholder about 1860.
(Muddy Creek Farm Library)

CHAPTER 27

Catherine

Susanna emptied her bucket of dishwater outside in the snow, as she watched the snow falling. She heard Peter Graf's horse coming up the trail. Peter would have no small business this time of the night.

Christian stood at the door waiting for Peter, who remained mounted, to speak.

"My news to all in your household concerns Catherine Eckerlin," he expressed solemnly.

A dart shot through Susanna. *Catherine, my dear sister, Catherine. If only Jacob would have gotten her out of there.* Susanna was tense with concern.

When everyone had gathered, Peter went on. "Catherine has expressed sorrow for leaving

An old clock owned by Emmanuel Byler, the first Amish bishop to settle in Big Valley, Pennsylvania. Christian Wenger owned a clock just like this one with only one weight. (Mifflin County Mennonite Historical Society)

113

the church and her husband. She never did believe Beissel's teaching, but was too proud to return and confess her sin. Christian, would you come with Brother Martin Graf and receive her back into fellowship and anoint her? She has asked for her family and Gabriel to come, too.

"Marie Sauer would welcome our presence and has urged us to come tonight. Catherine is very sick and probably doesn't have long to live. Marie said that Catherine certainly has the right to make decisions on her death bed."

Catherine die in that place! Susanna mourned. Then she remembered Catherine's words: "I will die a Mennonite." But all these years of misery when she could have come home and been useful in the Conestoga Valley . . .

Peter Graf left. Everyone scattered as they prepared to go. Susanna put on her wraps and stared into the fire. *What should she do?*

Christian Wenger hoisted the weight on the chain of his grandfather's clock. The clock struck seven with most beautiful cathedral-sounding chimes floating to every corner of the house. Whether it was a clock or simple a sundial, like most people owned, did not matter to Susanna.

Next, Christian laid all their axes on the raised hearth. Axe blades were warmed to prevent cracking in the cold weather. Slowly, he turned those axe handles that were lying on the mantle, being seasoned for use when needed.

Pushing the soapstone foot warmers toward the fire, Christian prepared for the night. Susanna's troubled face told him that now was the time.

Eighteen-year-old Susanna was miserable as her hatred toward Samuel Eckerlin had grown. She felt Christian's searching eyes on her. She was tired of feeling unhappy and was ready to do as he bid.

"Susanna, why aren't you in instruction class?" Christian asked.

With her eyes filling with tears, Susanna responded, "I can't bear Samuel; he took my sister away."

"Is it right to allow that to keep you from heaven?" Christian challenged her. "If God is to honor Catherine's anointing, each one present must have peace with God and man. Can you express peace if you are bitter toward Samuel? With God's help, you can decide to forgive him. Samuel is seeking for truth. We can't help him if we hate him. Will you forgive Samuel?"

Susanna promised willingly. Already she felt better after she had promised.

☩   ☩   ☩   ☩

The group shivered from the cold as Christian Wenger's horses pulled the sled through the deep blinding snow toward the convent. The women's cabins were dark except for a ribbon of light around

They shivered as Christian's horses pulled the sled through the deep blinding snow towards the convent.

the edge of Catherine's door. Magdelena Graf welcomed them as Veronica and Marie Sauer excused themselves. Veronica looked forsaken, just as Maria had said.

Soon Martin Graf, Grandfather and Grandmother Huber, Jacob Huber and his wife, and Marx and Aunt Anna Graf arrived. Susanna rejoiced as she realized it was the first time her family was all together; however, Samuel's absence left a vacancy in the small room.

After a short devotional, Christian asked Catherine questions which she answered with a nod, and she was restored to fellowship. Next, Martin read verses on healing in James 5 and asked each one to give his own testimony of peace.

Susanna felt humbled as she expressed peace. Nothing was too much for Catherine, or for her own soul. Brother Martin poured oil on Catherine's head, praying that God would grant healing if it be His will. As they prayed and sang, Catherine kept coughing. She asked Grandmother Huber and Magdelena to stay for the night; Marie Sauer and Veronica also returned. Between the four of them, Susanna knew that Catherine would have the best of care.

On the way home, Christian related instances where people were anointed and healed. For some it came slowly; others were healed immediately. If it were God's will not to heal, we must accept it.

"It is hard to see our sister suffer so much," Peter Ulrich cried.

"If she dies, she will be with our parents," Christopher comforted him. "I'm glad we could witness her being restored into fellowship and the anointing."

It was hard for Susanna to fall asleep that night. After Eve reminded her that God's grace was sufficient for this moment, Susanna slept.

The next morning Brother Martin Graf arrived. "I'm sorry, children, but God has seen it best to take Catherine home to be with Him. If you accept His will, you can rejoice in your sorrow," he encouraged them.

Susanna immediately went to her room and wept; however, she soon felt better as she thought about heaven and all that Catherine was enjoying.

Later, Christian took them to Grandfather's home where Jacob and Grandfather were making the casket. Friends from the community were digging the grave in the snow-covered ground. Catherine was to be buried beside her baby and Anna Eckerlin in the Grafs' family graveyard.

At the funeral the following day, Conestoga friends filled Grandfather's house. Veronica and Marie came from the convent; Samuel was absent. "His name is changed so he no longer claims Catherine," someone decided. Susanna wept silently. Catherine looked so frail in her white linen shroud.

Brother Herr had difficulty preaching. Tears flowed as family and friends grieved together. Susanna and her brothers pushed clumps of dirt down on top of the casket to help them know it was real. Catherine was gone, but they would see her again.

Later, when most of the people had gone, Marie Sauer told them about Catherine. Convent life had been too hard for her physically. Along with pneumonia, she had had tuberculosis. When Samuel had bought a large parcel of land near Emanuel's cabin, she had been concerned. From then on she no longer cared to live.

"Will you go with the Eicher girls?" Susanna overheard Magdelena ask Marie Sauer later. "Is it worth leaving your husband to have yourself appear morally corrupt to all Penn's Woods?"

Marie's face reddened. She did not answer.

"Thank you for sharing those things about Catherine with us," Magdelena expressed kindly.

"Apparently you have found fulfillment in the midst of your troubles in life," Marie approached Magdelena. "Have you no problems that are too hard to bear?"

"Yes, I have plenty of troubles, but God gives me grace. I feel wanted and needed by my adopted family in the Conestoga Valley. It was best not to run away but to face my problems squarely."

Marie looked closely at Magdelena. "I believe you," she said. "Your every move in life speaks of what you believe. Catherine should have done as you did."

"Don't wait too long to make that step yourself," Magdelena encouraged her. "I'm always here and ready to help."

"Thank you, Magdelena, and pray for me," Marie Sauer replied, and was gone.

Still later, when Susanna and Maria walked along the Horseshoe Trail, Maria shared what Grandmother had said. "We need to heed those who are anxious about whom we marry. Catherine was prayerful and careful about her marriage, yet she suffered long and hard. We can hardly afford to be as frivolous over marriage as some girls."

"Thank you for sharing," Susanna said. "Christian and Eve help me much, but there is no one like Grandmother to talk to."

"If Veronica Eberly leaves the convent, Grandfather and Grandmother plan to visit her. We can ask to go along," Maria suggested. "I'll miss the Eberly family if they move."

"Are you sure that you should care so much about Jacob Eberly?" Susanna wondered.

"I know," Maria responded. "Mother says that Gabriel and Jacob are with us like Samuel was, but things changed so fast. Jacob must prove himself a long time before I consider him. I'm moving to Aunt Anna's so that we don't see each other so much."

"Christian's sister, Elizabeth, is sick. He hopes she comes home before it is too late," Susanna added.

"Don't you mind that Gabriel is living at the Wengers?" Maria wondered.

"He is like a brother," Susanna replied.

"Catherine's life has reminded us that the best of men can go wrong. But, there is no reason to go the same road that she took," Maria said gravely.

Marx Graf's forge barn/blacksmith shop located midway between Farmersville and Bareville in Lancaster County, Pennsylvania.

CHAPTER 28

Gone To Hickorytown

Hurriedly, Susanna finished some last important tasks for Eve. *After dinner, Christopher and I will stop for Maria at Aunt Anna's and walk home to Hubers for the night. Tomorrow, we'll ride with Grandfather and Grandmother to Hickorytown to pay their taxes,* Susanna thought with anticipation.

Grandfather and Grandmother certainly must think it is very quiet with the Eberlys gone. We'll help fill their cabin for one night, and on the way Maria will tell us how it happened.

Susanna liked to visit Aunt Anna. When Marx wasn't in his shop, he worked on their new cabin. Susanna lifted her skirts and slipped through Marx's stone grike. *Our dream of sliding through a grike to travel to Hickorytown is being fulfilled*, she remembered.

"Marx has a pile of fine oak logs on the rails for spring seasoning," Christopher mentioned. "Aunt Anna is eager to have a floor in their cabin."

A chimney built of clay and sticks rose high above the roof of the forge barn. Through the open door, Susanna saw the forge with the bellows. A tub of water used to cool the iron sat next to the anvil.

The stack of iron rods in one corner would be melted into all kinds of tools. Marx's workbench held chisel axes, broad axes to square logs, a post axe to cut mortices and tenons in corner logs, and split axes to make fence posts. There were frows to split shingles and barrel staves. Forks, rakes, and hoes leaned against the wall. From long pegs hung mill dogs, hewing dogs, and sawing dogs, which were used to clamp down the logs when they worked on them. Next to a grinding stone were knives, scythes, sickles, and saws, and an eight-foot framed pit saw that was used to square beams.

"These iron tools make work much easier for us," Christopher remarked. "Joel, who lives on the Welsh Mountain, works with

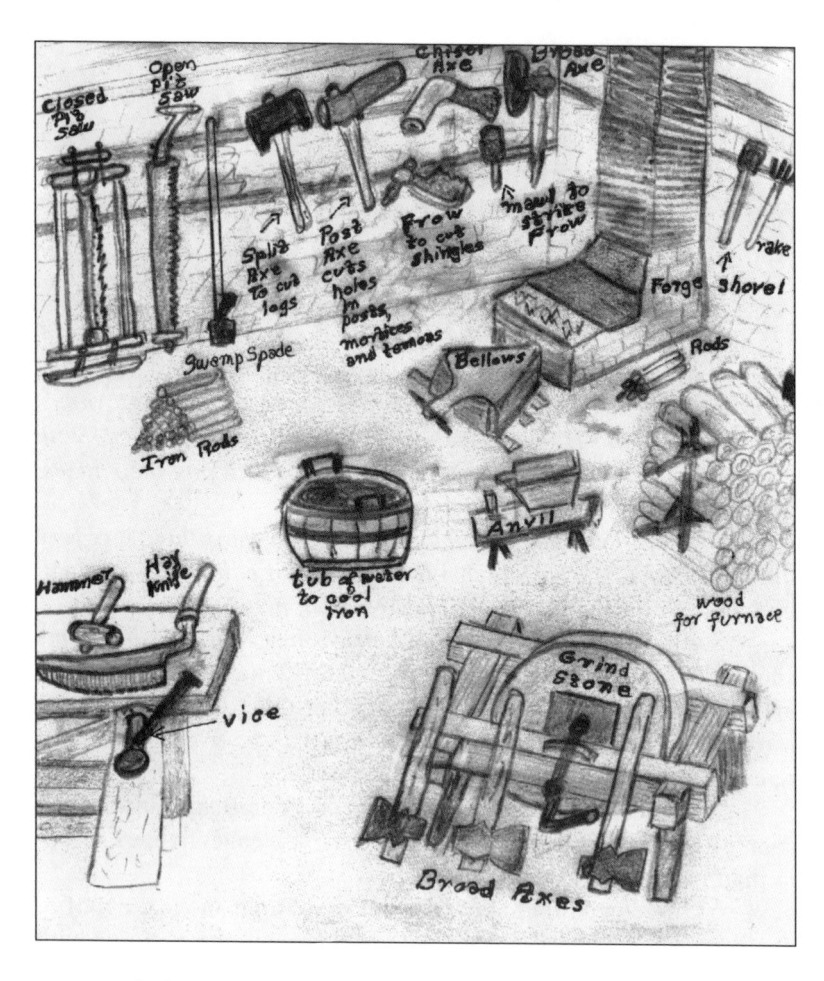

"These iron tools make work much easier for us."

iron, too. There is a larger market for tools than both Marx and he can produce."

Daisy the cow bellowed a friendly welcome from her window in the barn. "The locusts ate your grain last year so you are starving on hay. This is April. Surely you'll graze on new grass soon." As Christopher and Susanna walked toward the cabin, Daisy accepted Susanna's information with another loud bellow.

After saying a quick hello and good-bye to Aunt Anna, the group was on its way.

"The Eberlys missed this trip. They are gone!" Maria announced.

"How did it happen?" Susanna was eager to know.

"One afternoon our deacon visited Jacob Eberly and Grandfather. That evening Jacob brought Veronica to Grandfather's home. She exchanged her Quaker robe for Aunt Anna's dress and Jacob returned it to Marie Sauer with a note. The note said that she was leaving Beissel's false teaching and the convent for good. All she brought along was her bread bowl and some pear seeds she had saved.

"I gave Veronica my new shawl and bonnet. Marx and Aunt Anna bought all of them new Germantown-made stockings and boots that they had purchased for the occasion."

"Will she fit in with a family of Mennonite children?" Christopher asked.

"Hardly. It will be hard for Veronica to tend a family of teenagers. After not knowing her for eight years, the children wonder if they can trust her."

At dusk, Martin Graf brought a horse and wagon. The wagon was loaded with food, a spinning wheel, material, seeds, tools, needles—everything she could possibly need during the summer. She and her children stood there spellbound. Martin handed the reins and some money to Jacob and said, "God bless you, brother, and keep you. When you find your new home, we'll come to see you."

Jacob said, "Thank you," but he could say no more.

Veronica said, "Say thank you to whoever gave it, and pray for us!" Then she wept.

Brother Martin shook hands with each of the children and encouraged them to help their mother and Jacob. They looked fearful.

"Will Veronica attend our meetings at Hammer Creek?" Christopher asked.

"She says they will attend," Maria said. "They stayed at Grandfather's house that night and left for Hickorytown the next morning. They have gone to Hickorytown, and we are going, too. Grandfather wants to get there so he can be sure they are on their way."

"Hickorytown has only 100 people living there. The largest town around here is Saeue Schwamm," Christopher said, as the schwamm came into view.

"There are twenty cabins in a row along the north side of the schwamm and more scattered elsewhere," Maria figured.

"The new arrivals are Rancks, Wolfs, Sprechers, Brimmers, Winters, Mummas, and Rudys. Three years ago Rev. Stoever, their minister, baptized the first babies in the Lutheran Church."

Maria went to Jacob's house for the night; the others went to Grandfather's.

In the morning they climbed on Grandfather's wagon, and the trip began. Bright Star joined them on the Horseshoe Trail.

"We should remember to call Hickorytown by its new name, Lancaster," Maria reminded them. "Saeue Schwamm should be called Earltown, also."

They followed wheel tracks in and around the forest trees beside the narrow foot trail. A path disappeared into a clearing where a Rohrer family lived.

Later, the wagon followed the deep, swift water of the Conestoga. "This was nothing like the Schuylkill River," Susanna decided. When they came to a ford at a more shallow place, Christopher handed a pole to Bright Star. Further downstream, wheel ruts went up the opposite bank. Christopher and Bright Star would push the wagon to that point.

Water splashed against the wagon wheels as they moved forward in the wet sand. There was more splashing as the wheels scraped the creek stones.

Suddenly, the wagon lifted, swayed a bit, and then stabilized. "We are sailing!" Christopher shouted with delight.

Gracefully, Bright Star dropped her pole into the creek bottom and pushed as if she enjoyed it immensely. Then the wagon jerked as its wheels again struck stones. The wheels clattered until they followed the oxen up over the bank. Their wet sides glistened in the morning sunlight.

"That was mild," Grandfather assured them, and Susanna knew why.

Sometimes drivers left their wagons midstream and swam to the front of their oxen or horses. There, with soft words, they would coax the frightened animals toward the opposite shore.

Witmer's low land between the creek and Hickorytown was full of ruts and potholes. Gracefully, the oxen moved across them and didn't stumble once.

Nearby, an Indian woman carried a willow basket on her shoulders. The basket was decorated with beads and feathers and probably held meal.

Another woman looked at Bright Star strangely and waved. Her baby smiled at them from a fur-lined basket on his mother's shoulder. "That way a mother can work and hold her baby too," Bright Star explained.

Beyond them were children playing near wigwams. Next was the spring and the hickory tree where treaties were made. Further up the path stood twelve poorly kept cabins. "Those cabins are old and have changed ownership many times," Grandfather explained. A sign at the next larger cabin read, "Postlewaite's Tavern." At another cabin Grandfather paid his taxes. He learned that the Eberlys had left for their purchased land which was between Ebys and Indiantown.

"Now, to Brother Hershi's for the night," Grandfather informed them. They followed more wagon tracks around stately trees, and then forded the Little Conestoga Creek. Finally, they arrived at a large cabin surrounded with a beautiful stone wall. In the pasture horses lifted their heads to see who was coming.

The travelers followed a smooth lane to the cabin and unloaded the wagon. A hired man took the horses and wagon to the stone barn for the night. Susanna soon learned that travelers and old-time friends, like Grandfather, always received a hearty welcome.

After visiting, they talked among themselves in the comfortable bedroom. Bright Star touched the beautiful braided rug and colorful patchwork quilt. She sat on the chest to warm her feet at a foot stove heater. Through the hole in the metal grate, she saw the hot charcoal. A burning candle inside an iron lantern provided light while baskets of dried tea and flowers decorating the room gave a pleasing aroma.

"This is such a fine house," Maria whispered to Grandmother.

"Yes, there are prosperous Mennonites in these parts. Settlers in the Conestoga Valley will catch up with them in another ten years," Grandmother explained.

"Beissel would never agree to such fine things," Bright Star commented as she looked questionably at Grandmother.

"God wants us to enjoy the fruits of our labor; yet we are to live simply," Grandmother answered. "We must seek guidance as to where simplicity stops and luxury begins. It is hard for a rich man to enter heaven because of what riches do to a person. God would have us share our riches like the Hershis are doing with us.

"Christian Eby built a ninety-nine-foot barn. That was his limit for now because he felt we were prospering too fast in the Conestoga Valley. It takes things like that to slow us down.

"In the morning you may come to our room to dress by the warm stove. There's a chair in there that rocks like a cradle," Grandmother smiled.

The next morning the travelers carried Sister Hershi's foot warmers into the new meetinghouse. Even though it was cold, with Grandmother's lap robe tucked around them and the foot warmers, they were warm.

In Brother Hershi's message, he reminded them to pray for their brethren who were still en route to America. Another ship had arrived from Holland after twenty-four weeks on the sea. Two-thirds of the passengers had died from hunger and thirst.

"So, more white people keep coming and we're driving the Indians further west," Susanna said, trying to imagine what Bright Star must be thinking. "The Indians, Negroes, and we white Anabaptists are all people without a country. Life is not equal because men are greedy."

"Welcome to Conestoga Valley's paradise," Quick Foot hailed them later as they returned on the Horseshoe Trail

He is feeling good about this place, Susanna decided.

"Grandfather and Grandmother acted so young today," Christopher commented later. "They are likely relieved about the Eberlys going to Hickorytown to buy a house. I hope none of us ever follows Beissel."

"It won't be me," Susanna declared.

Chapter 29

No Grain

March winds had brought April showers. April showers had brought May flowers, followed by a long heat wave without rain. Now the grass was brown; bean stalks were yellow and infested with bugs; and the wheat growth was stunted.

"Here they come," Maria announced as Marx and Peter Graf arrived with a pack of six horses, loaded with the Eberlys' provisions. Grandfather and Grandmother followed in their small wagon while Christian and Gabriel mounted their horses which seemed to be impatient to leave.

"Find a corner in the wagon," Grandfather instructed Susanna, Maria, and Bright Star.

"It will be another hot day, but we'll ford enough creeks where we can wade and have a drink," Grandmother predicted.

After crossing a ridge and fording the Conestoga Creek, they were soon following the Cocalico Creek. They came to the place where a Zug family lived in a mill which they were building. "Their son is with the Fathers of the Desert," Peter Graf informed them.

Gabriel came riding from upstream and reported that the water in Middle Creek, which emptied into the Cocalico, was low. "The Eberlys' spring flows into Middle Creek," he reminded them. "It must be very dry up there."

After fording Hammer Creek, the group noticed that the trail had become very rough. The men gave their horses to the girls and Grandmother so they could ride easier and travel faster.

By noon, they came to Ebys' cabin. Christian's wife, Elizabeth, welcomed the girls warmly. "I've wished to see you again. You were the only girls from the Conestoga Valley who witnessed our wedding. Remember?"

"How could we forget?" Maria quickly responded. "Your wedding was a very important day in our lives."

"I thought you were the most happily married couple," Susanna added. "But maybe the couple hiding in the barrels were more grateful."

"Remember the one long fascinating street in Germantown and the glorious and painful sights in Philadelphia?" Elizabeth reminded them.

"The Eberlys need the food badly," the Ebys told them. "When it was time to plow, Jacob sprained his ankle; however, with his determination and his brother's help, the crops were planted. Their ground was drier than ours.

"The Eberlys and Quick Foot's brothers and their families come faithfully to our meetings. A young couple—John Erb, who married Barbara Johns—also comes. Barbara's father, who is Amish, mapped out on paper his ideal plan for a perfect town. He'll likely build a town someday named Johnstown.

"They say that two other Amish families arrived with them—the Jacob Masts and Jacob Bergeys. They are settling east of Weber Thal."

"Christian started building a mill a year ago, but now there's no grain to grind," Elizabeth remarked.

"There will be better years ahead," Grandmother assured her. "Grandfather's and my aching bones say rain will come."

"We'd better move on to the Eberlys so that we don't get soaked," Marx suggested. "The sooner we can give them a good meal, the better."

As they followed the trail east toward Indiantown, they neared one of the distant mountains which Susanna had seen from Magdelena's lookout. "Veronica lives near the Black Ridge of South Mountain," Peter Graf told them.

"Middle Creek is ahead. Get a drink and cool your feet, and two more miles will bring us to the Eberlys," Marx directed.

Further on, Grandfather noted that the leaves were hanging limply. Even the hardiest weeds were brown. Suddenly he cheered, "Praise the Lord! I see a dark cloud with a cobwebby sky behind. Let us stop and pray that rain will come." With the needs of their dear ones at heart, they asked the Lord for rain.

Seeing the Eberly cabin ahead, Peter Graf observed aloud, "It is a good beginning." The logs were laid on a foundation of stone.

An enormous white oak tree shaded the cabin's roof and the spring beside it.

Suddenly, the curious faces at the door brightened, and in the next instant Ulrich was in the wagon beside Grandfather. Grandmother hurriedly crawled down off the wagon and drew the girls close to her.

"You've come!" Jacob spoke for himself and his brothers as they gathered around Grandfather and Grandmother.

Grandmother looked beyond her beloved children to Veronica who stood watching. "Veronica, it is good to see you here with your children," Grandmother greeted her warmly. Veronica's stiff composure melted with Grandmother's kind, friendly nature.

"You have a well-built cabin," Grandfather praised them. "Though your crops are planted, the good Lord has withheld the rain."

"Yes, Christian Eby and John Wissler helped us build it. The boys did well this spring, but it is discouraging as we wait for rain," Veronica replied.

"We heard it was very dry up here so we've brought you some food," Grandfather told them.

The Eberlys' eyes filled with tears. "Thank you," Veronica cried. "Our food is as well as gone. Every few days, Quick Foot's brothers bring enough food for a few days. There's no more wild life here anymore. Indiantown had rains that did not come here, so they have food to spare."

"If they have no more food, they say, 'Quick Foot will bring more.' What about the red man caring for the white man? If I run from the Mennonites, the Indians will find me," she spoke frankly.

"We'd like you to come back into our fellowship," Christian prompted her.

"I'm slowly coming, Brother Wenger," Veronica assured him. "I'll never go back to Beissel's false doctrine again."

There was a sigh of relief when Veronica said that. The uncertainty about the direction which she would go was cleared.

"Praise the Lord! Don't stay away too long," Christian encouraged her. The matter was dropped.

"Did we buy land at the wrong place?" Jacob asked.

"It took good soil and years of rain to grow your giant oak tree," Marx insisted.

"This soil has much clay in it," Jacob explained.

"I'll tell you how to build this soil before we go," Marx assured him.

"Here are some bean seeds," Veronica rejoiced aloud. "If it rains today, I'll plant the seeds tomorrow so that we'll have beans by September."

A flash of lightning and a crack of thunder alerted everyone. Immediately, they put everything into the cabin. The horses were tied in the temporary stable which Jacob had built.

The rain came and the air became fresh. Suddenly, every green thing came to life. As they watched the storm pass, Grandmother set a meal on the table—ham, cheese, schnitz pies, milk, and freshly baked bread with strawberry jelly.

As the Eberlys ate, the others just nibbled. "Eat more," Veronica coaxed.

"No, we've had enough," Christian insisted.

After the rain, the men found a spot in the barn to spend the night, and the girls and women slept inside on the Eberlys' comfortable ticks.

In the morning, the aroma of frying bacon and scrapple filled the cabin. After planting the bean seeds, the men cut mortices and tenons on beams which Jacob had squared for a larger barn using the tools Marx had sharpened. Gabriel was finishing the walls for the springhouse, and Grandfather was preparing to lay the roof shingles and put the door in place.

Before dinner, the travelers bid good-bye and were on their way.

"Grandfather, is it true that Israel wants Gabriel to help him build a new cabin?" Maria asked on the way home.

"Yes, and Gabriel wants to help his brothers grow spiritually. The ministers have warned him plainly that trouble lies ahead if he goes by himself," Grandfather replied.

"I'm hungry. I couldn't eat in front of the hungry Eberlys," Maria exclaimed.

"Thank God, the rain will bring food," Susanna rejoiced.

CHAPTER 30

Vengeance

In February 1734, Gabriel left the Mennonites to help Israel build another cabin close to Beissel. By then, the area around Beissel and the Fathers of the Desert was called the Settlement of the Solitary. Gabriel had gone to the settlement against everyone's advice, and he was missed sorely by the Wengers.

The others were in constant prayer for Gabriel, sometimes with fasting.

Later, in June of the same year, Susanna unhooked the door of the ground cellar. Something was amiss. Looking closer, she noticed that the apples, the last barrel of vinegar, and the schnitz pies were gone! She searched for tracks but found none. The cloth and string were removed from the remaining crock of apple butter. There was an indentation in the apple butter which Susanna assumed meant that someone had taken a lick.

"What's going on in here?" Gabriel asked, coming into the cellar.

"Oh! You're here!" Susanna exclaimed in surprise.

"Eve sent me down to see what was taking you so long. Why are you standing here, gaping as if you lost your best friend?"

"I didn't lose my best friend, but we've lost the best part of our supper. The schnitz pies, plus much more, are gone."

"Did you find any tracks?" he asked.

"None," Susanna replied. "We worked so hard to make the schnitz pies for tonight and Sunday."

"It was likely the Indians," Gabriel decided. "The locusts ate their food last year, and it's dry again this year. They are hungry."

"They could ask for food," Susanna insisted.

"Some Indians still think this place belongs to them," Gabriel reminded her. "Even though Penn has been honest, they accuse him of stealing their land, so they assume that what the land produces belongs to them. Hopefully they won't take vengeance because of so many new settlers."

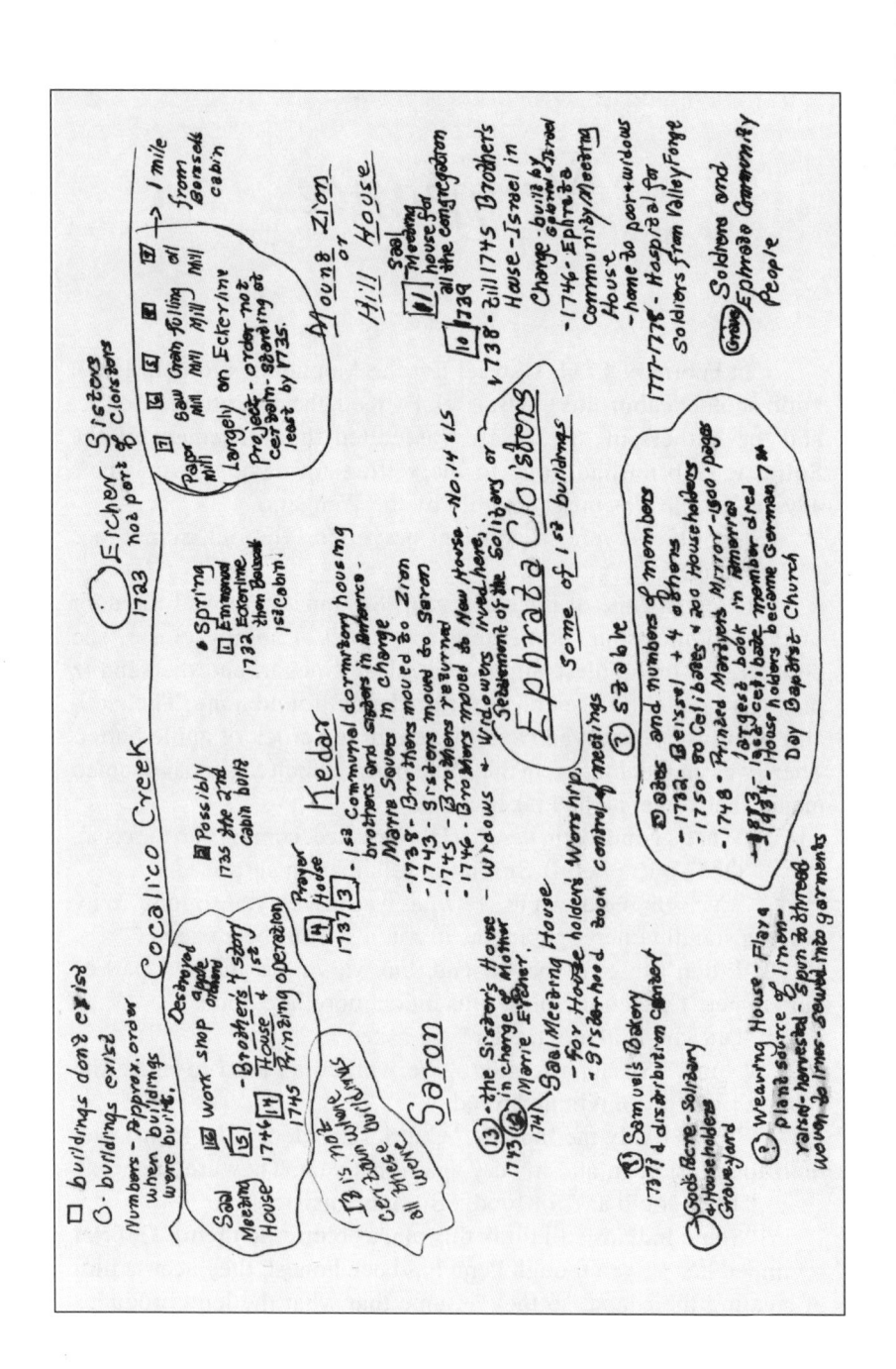

[Handwritten notes page — rotated 90°, transcribed in reading order]

Legend
- □ buildings don't exist
- ○ buildings exist
- Numbers - approx. order when buildings were built
- [B] It is not known where certain buildings were

Ercher Sisters — 1723 — not part of Cloisters

Cocalico Creek

- [12] Paper Mill
- [12] Saw Mill
- [12] Grain Mill
- [12] Fulling Mill
- [12] Oil Mill
- Largely on Eckerline Project - order not certain - standing at least by 1735.
- → 1 mile from Beissel's cabin

● Spring
□ 1732 Emmanuel Eckerline then Beissel 1st cabin
□ Possibly 1735 the 2nd cabin built

Kedar
- Prayer House [4] 1737
- [3] 1st Communal dormitory housing - brothers and sisters in Ephrata - Marie Sauer in charge
  - 1738 - Brothers moved to Zion
  - 1743 - Sisters moved to Saron
  - 1745 - Brothers returned
  - 1746 - Brothers moved to New House - No. 14 & 15
  - Widows & Widowers lived here - Settlement of the Solitary or

Saron
- Saal Meeting House [5] work shop - Destroyed apple orchard
- [6] Brothers' 4 story House 4 1st J 1744 Printing operation
- (13) The Sister's House 1743 in charge of Mother Marie Eicher.
- Saal Meeting House 1741 - For House holders Worship - Sisterhood Book control of meetings

Ephrata Cloisters — Some of 1st buildings

- ? Stable

② Dates and numbers of members
- 1732 - Beissel + 4 others
- 1750 - 80 Celibates & 200 Households
- 1748 - Printed Martyrs Mirror - 1500 pages largest book in America
- 1813 - last celibate member died
- 1934 - House holders become German 7th Day Baptist Church

Mount Zion / Hill House
- Saal Meeting [11] house for all the congregation [10] 1739
- √1738 - [11] 1745 Brothers House-Israel in charge - built by General Israel
- 1746 - Ephrata Community/Moravian House
- home to poor + widows
- 1777-1778 - Hospital for soldiers from Valley Forge

○ Soldiers and
○ Ephrata Community People

○ God's Acre - Solitary & Householders Graveyard

[15] Samuel's Bakery 1737? & distribution center

⑨ Weaving House - Flax plant source of linen - raised - harvested. Spun to thread - woven to linen - sewed into garments

"I thought you were at the Settlement of the Solitary. What are you doing here?" Susanna asked. "You were baptized and renamed Jothan. Where is your white robe? Did you finish building your cabin?"

"Yes, it is finished. I built it almost by myself while Israel went preaching," Gabriel told her. "Israel kept me as long as he could. Beissel baptized me and renamed me Jothan, to my regret. I've come home in a buckskin jacket. Christian said that I may stay if I don't influence anyone wrongly."

Susanna almost cried for joy over Gabriel's return. The circle around the table would again be complete.

"Israel will probably live in his house," Susanna supposed aloud.

"A householder is living there," he informed her. "Soon they will have love feasts and meetings in part of it. They call it the Hill House."

Together Susanna and Gabriel left the ground cellar and went into the cabin where they met Christian Wenger.

"How did Samuel's bake house go this winter?" Christian asked Gabriel.

"The rich people donated so much grain that Samuel built a granary," Gabriel answered. "They think it is righteous to feed their surplus to the poor. The poor went hungry rather than eat Beissel's bread, so Beissel's followers ate it."

"Why did Beissel leave the German Baptists?" Christian asked.

"He never said why," Gabriel replied. "Beissel wants the freedom to live as humbly as possible, and to attract others to do likewise. He has not learned that a spiritual group needs rules. Also, they must be able to feed themselves.

"Last winter the brethren were bored and some talked of leaving until Beissel decided to give them some work. In freezing weather, he had them dig up clay and make it pliable enough to fill the cracks in his cabin walls. The brethren complained bitterly about that and their meager fare.

"Israel used this opportunity to win Beissel's approval by ridiculing the brethren for doing the job poorly. They became angry and thought about leaving. Next, Israel sent them to help me with the Hill House. The brethren complained, afraid they would need to do the plowing next. They despise him. Beissel doesn't like the way Israel makes the brethren work, but he likes Israel too well to make him do differently."

"True love makes rules and, in kindness, requires obedience as well," Christian reminded Gabriel.

"You're right," Gabriel agreed. "Rather than offending with rules, Beissel seeks to win others by his example. When that fails, he asks them to find clay in freezing weather. He isn't consistent."

"Beissel knows that my brother's goal is to make the settlement a place of business. He has different ideas, but he will not stop their money making."

"Smoke!" Peter shouted. The men ran out the door, knowing it was too dry to start a fire. In the north, clouds of black smoke roared into the sky. It moved with the wind northeast toward the settlement. With fire-fighting tools in hand, they jumped on their horses and sped in that direction. The men living in solitude followed.

"May I go, too?" Susanna asked Eve.

"Unless the wind changes, you'll be safe," Eve gave permission, and Susanna rode the remaining horse toward the smoke, which was moving closer to the Settlement of the Solitary.

Susanna crossed over the ridge and the Conestoga Creek. Ahead of her, near a Mennonite settler's cabin, she saw where the fire appeared to have started. The trees and brush were burning and smoking. She greeted the settler's wife and some Indian squaws who were forced to leave their homes due to the smoke. Stopping at the river, the fire headed east. Several Indians were trying to keep the fire from spreading.

"What started it?" Susanna asked.

"The solitary brethren are blaming us," a Mennonite woman replied. "My husband, who forbade them to come here because of their false doctrine, is at the settlement fighting the fire. Too many lives are in danger there."

"Some blame us," one of the squaws added in broken German. "Too many white men make Indians unhappy. No place to hunt and grow food."

"People from other places are settling at every spring and creek, waiting for the salvation of the Lord, whatever that means," the Mennonite woman said. "We Mennonites on this side of the Conestoga Creek hoped to make a Mennonite settlement where we would have land for our children, but they've filled every corner around us."

"Recently, Deacon Frantz laid a rail on the barn hill at Long's barn. Everyone who was for Beissel was told to step on one side of the rail. Those who wished to be German Baptists were to step on the other side. After decisions were made, he told everyone to attend only their own meetings from that time on. Beissel's men left, saying something about judgment that would come.

"No one around here agrees with Beissel. Since the dignitaries have arrived, we wonder how much space the settlement will need."

Two men followed the creek toward them. They had burns and were overcome from the smoke. As the women treated their burns and gave them a drink of water, they began talking.

"The new ferry on the Schuylkill River and the improved King's Highway is drawing the wrong kind of people to the Conestoga Valley," the one man said. "When Hans Graf surveyed the King's Highway, he probably had no idea who it would bring. The working people who cleared the wilderness are being pushed west."

"Hans will soon have the road from Lancaster to Harris Ferry surveyed. Then we'll be able to go west," the other man said to cheer him. "At least we did our Christian duty by turning the fire away from the settlement. Every Mennonite, Lutheran, German Baptist, and Indian who saw the smoke came to help. The fire destroyed one of the householders' barns and almost took his cabin. The wind has died down, so they should soon be able to stop the fire."

"Magdelena is busy helping some who were burned or overcome with smoke," the first man added.

Susanna hurried home to Eve and then on to Magdelena.

"We'll probably never be sure who started that fire, but it looks as though it was directed toward the settlement," Magdelena told Susanna.

"In Romans 12:19, it says, 'Vengeance is mine; I will repay, saith the Lord,'" Susanna said. "One wrong hardly makes another right. You have so many injured people to care for. May I come and help you awhile?"

Christian gave Susanna permission to stay at Magdelena's home, and she did.

CHAPTER 31

Whited Sepulcher

It was June. With her Indian-made brush, Susanna whitewashed the trunk of every oak tree around the Wenger cabin where she was staying. Yesterday, she had whitened both the outside and inside walls of the ground cellar and springhouse, and the inside of the cabin. Whitewashing brightened the corners and made the rooms friendly and inviting.

Susanna had poured many scoops of hot coals into the iron kettle of boiling water. The ashes popped, sizzled, and steamed, finally thickening the water into paste as she stirred it with a six-foot pole. When it became too thick, it was diluted with water until it was thin enough. This white paste was poured into a bucket, more water was added, and it was ready to be used for another day of whitening every corner.

"Are you ready to get smeared with whitewash again today?" Christopher asked from behind her. "Did you whitewash that stump up there in the field where Gabriel is plowing?" Christopher pointed toward the strangest thing Susanna had ever seen.

"No. Why would I bother painting a stump up there?" Susanna asked.

"It looks like one of those rich men's tombstones in Philadelphia, but it's much smaller. I'm going to see what it is," Christopher decided. He jumped over the fence and ran in that direction.

Susanna watched Gabriel guide his plow away from the white object and toward the opposite end of the field. Had he seen the *thing*?

Her brother Peter was coming from another direction to see what it was. He and Christopher, reaching the object at the same time, just stood and looked at it.

The thing must be dead because they aren't kicking it, Susanna decided. Then the object moved, turned, and faced them. It was a person draped in a long, white robe with a hood over his head. Susanna waited and watched. The person in white had apparently come to see Gabriel, because he began walking in his direction.

Christopher soon returned and told her that it was their brother-in-law, Samuel Eckerlin. "The Quakers didn't like it that Samuel chose their garb, so Samuel designed one of his own. He calls it the special garb of the order.

"A while back, Jan Neily, one of the celibate brethren, had become insane. After he broke into a house during the night, Beissel's brethren didn't trust to leave their wives alone, lest he break in on them. Jan then ran to Philadelphia and climbed up to the courthouse bell. There he made such a commotion that a large crowd of people came together. He wanted to stir up the people against Beissel. Later, he regained his right mind and became Beissel's baker.

"The Quakers didn't wish to have people of that sort dressing in their garb."

"Doesn't it bother you when Samuel comes around here so much?" Susanna asked.

"He doesn't bother me, but I fear he may persuade Gabriel to go with him," Christopher responded.

"I can't forget that he took our sister away," Susanna admitted. "If she hadn't married him, she would not have joined Beissel."

"It was Catherine's choice, as well as Samuel's, to enter the solitary life," Christopher informed her. "I'm not wasting my time brooding over them. I've forgiven Samuel, and he knows he'll never persuade me to follow his way. You may as well forgive and forget, too, Susanna.

"Oh, I forgot to tell you! Christian wants you to go in and hold the baby while Eve rests," Christopher added. "You'd better wash before you go. You were almost as white as Samuel. Peter says that Samuel reminds him of a whited sepulcher."

Susanna hurried toward Graf's Run, which was nearby, to see how bad she looked and to wash. After she had changed her clothes, she was ready to hold the day-old infant.

"You may hold little Hans," Christian said, handing her the small bundle. "Magdelena said he must stay warm. Keep his blanket wrapped snugly around him." Christian disappeared into the other room.

That evening, after supper, Peter announced that Samuel was conducting a singing with Beissel's new hymn book. Samuel had edited the book and persuaded Ben Franklin of Philadelphia to print it along with a weekly German newspaper.

"Do you expect to attend?" Christopher asked, as he greased his boots to soften the hide.

"No, Christopher. Their songs are different than those which we sing in the *Ausbund*," Peter replied seriously. "Sauer says that the words to Beissel's songs make Beissel a Christ. I asked Samuel about that and he asked, 'Is there anything wrong with another Christ?'"

"The Scripture says in Isaiah 45:21: 'I am a just God and a Saviour; there is none else beside me,'" Christian immediately reminded them.

"What is the meaning of Samuel's white garb?" Christopher asked.

"Samuel and the other celibate brethren can sit in jail for a week and sing praises. That doesn't justify their disobedience to the laws, no matter what they wear," Peter reasoned.

"If it was an error for the apostolic Christians to worship on the first day of the week, the Scriptures would tell us so," Christian instructed them. "Samuel's work on Sunday was twice at fault: once for not following New Testament teaching and again for disobeying civil laws. There is no reward in suffering for one's wrongs."

"When work at the mill is slow, Gabriel lives here. Will he be a bad influence on us?" Peter asked.

Christian kept oiling the harnesses scattered on the floor about him. "Gabriel is struggling to think right." Christian's answer was thoughtful. "At his baptism he vowed to be a part of us. Our prayers will work like this oil to keep him pliable and running smoothly. Yes, if he fails, I fear his influence on us; but we can't turn him away at this point."

"What can we do to encourage Gabriel?" Christopher wanted to know.

"Peter says that Samuel reminds him of a whited sepulcher," Christian reminded them. "Our modest, simple clothes will complement our holy life within. But it takes both a sanctified outward appearance and a holy heart to convince the world of truth. Only when leaders properly guide our people into such living can we convince others."

"Samuel doubts that any leader can totally submit to other leaders," Peter offered.

"I don't always agree with our leaders on all issues," Christian admitted. "But once a decision is made, I submit to it and support the action of the group. This keeps us in line when our opinions aren't always the best.

"As a horse without a harness is useless, so Christians without spiritual leadership are prone to error," Christian warned them. "We can influence many with our convictions, but without submission to one another, what will the end be?"

"Gabriel must feel very alone at times," Peter sympathized. "He is the only Eckerlin who is submitting to anyone."

"If he sees any of us chaffing under our discipline, we may discourage him. Can we be a perfectly submitted family?" Christian challenged them.

Susanna didn't want to be a whited sepulcher. She wanted to submit.

Chapter 32

After The Storm

At the end of the summer, Susanna joined the harvesters. She refreshed herself with a drink from the spot where Hammer Creek emptied into the Cocalico Creek. This time they were going to the Eberlys to harvest wheat. They had just passed Long's barn on the bank of the creek.

"One year we had locusts and then a dry spell. This year we have a heat wave. Drink plenty and work slowly," Christian reminded them. "Already, too many have died of sunstroke in the field."

"Last week Martin Graf stopped his work to help a family bury their son," Peter Graf informed them. "Everyone knows the path to the kindhearted deacon when they need someone to give the last rites. I'm glad we harvested Brother Martin's wheat yesterday."

The harvesters mounted and turned their horses up over the river bank and took a shortcut through the loop of the Cocalico. To their right was the race that a settler had dug for a mill. A herd of deer grazed in the shaded far side of the grassland. The low pasture was surrounded with tree-clad hills.

"It is cooler in this low place. I'd love to stay here!" Gabriel wished. Peter and Christian agreed. Susanna removed the long thorn which fastened her bark knapsack and gave each of them a piece of dried venison and a schnitz pie.

"This settler needs help to finish his wall," Gabriel nodded toward the unfinished stone foundation for a mill.

Behind the race was a sea of blue flowers on a field of flax. Next was a field of red clover. Behind that a mass of pink hollyhocks and lilies almost obscured the door to an underground shelter.

"What a lovely place to live!" Susanna exclaimed.

"With Hammer Creek and Middle Creek both flowing into this loop of the Cocalico, this low place is flooded during heavy rains. It wouldn't be very nice then," Peter commented seriously.

When they were finished eating, they crossed the pasture to the place where the Middle Creek emptied into the Cocalico Creek.

As they climbed the creek bed which went uphill, the intense heat penetrated through the canopy of leaves above them.

Arriving at the Eberlys, the group found Veronica's boys exhausted and eager for help. The men slept and refreshed themselves near the spring.

Harvesting began early the next day since there was no dew on the ground. With their sickles, Jacob and his brothers helped the men cut the wheat and rake it with wooden forks into orderly piles. Maria and Susanna bound the stalks into sheaves and stood them up into shocks. If the women lagged behind, the young men helped them. They worked slowly in the intense heat, drinking from the buckets of water which Veronica supplied.

Suddenly, Gabriel fell to the ground, screaming. The men hastily picked him up and carried him to the spring. Thrashing his arms and legs wildly, they knew he was confused by the things he was saying. As they covered him with wet rags, Christian prayed, asking God to spare his life.

For what seemed like a long time, they kept wetting him with cold water from the spring. Gradually, his convulsions lessened and he lay still. Occasionally, they would start again, but finally, they ceased.

"Where am I?" Gabriel asked anxiously.

"You'll be all right," Christian assured him. "You had a heat stroke."

"Yes, I remember now," Gabriel replied. "I feel better now," he said, trying to get up, but at Christian's orders, Gabriel rested while the others returned to the field.

They worked slowly in the heat, hoping they would soon be finished.

"We're finished!" Peter Graf shouted, pointing to the fast moving clouds. "Look at the trees swaying. Feel the cool wind." Holding up their arms, they welcomed the cool breeze.

"Head for the cabin!" Christian warned as they saw the rain coming across the field toward them. Susanna could hardly run with the pouring rain and the wind lashing against her. The bright streaks of lightning and loud claps of thunder drove her on.

Maria stumbled and fell beside her. "What is wrong?" Susanna yelled.

"I've overturned my ankle," she moaned, pain written on her face as she held it.

Unexpectedly, Marx grabbed the frightened girl and carried her into the cabin.

Peter grabbed Susanna's hand. "Here, I'll help you," he offered. Marx put a splint on Maria's ankle and encouraged her to keep her foot elevated. Gabriel, still looking pale, was up and watching the storm. The storm raged for a long time. "This wind is strong enough to remove roofs and level buildings," Christian observed. "Never have I seen such a storm."

At last the storm ended and the sun shone brightly. Checking the sun dial, which read eight o'clock, they realized the storm had raged for an hour. They straightened the leaning shocks and headed to Jacob's hay field.

Gabriel and Peter replaced a pole frame on the hay rick. Susanna handed them the wooden shingles as they fastened them to the frame. Each stack was round at the top and looked like an inverted bell, which helped to protect them from pouring rain.

"Jacob stacks hay with the skill of an experienced farmer," Peter commented. "It took his know-how to hold these ricks together through such a storm."

"Jacob does his work right. He learned much from Grandfather," Susanna reminded Peter.

Evening came and the moon shone brightly around Jacob's hay ricks. As Jacob brought their supper toward them in a stone boat, Gabriel cut chunks of dry hay from the rick to sit on. The stone boat served as their table. Times like this were refreshing after their hard work.

The following day, before they left, Veronica said, "Sometimes it takes storms to sift us. I still struggle to free myself from the false teaching, but I've decided to come back to the church."

"Thank God! If it took a storm in your heart or a storm like we just had to decide this, thanks be to Him!" Christian rejoiced aloud. "We will be praying for you as you work things out with your bishop. We have longed to see you take this step."

"I have struggled with hatred toward Samuel for so long, but that storm is past too," Susanna recalled. "I felt better after I forgave him, and I am happier since I was baptized." Never would she forget the moment of solemnity when Brother Herr poured water over her head. It was her way of saying that her heart was right with God and giving her loyalty to the Mennonites.

She wished Gabriel would end his battle by consenting to stay with them. If only he would submit. She, her brothers, and Christian and Eve were trying their best to help Gabriel.

Jacob's hay rick withstood the storm, and, with God's help, all of us can withstand the storms we may face. Susanna felt reassured.

CHAPTER 33

Strange Powers

After the harvest, Peter Ulrich married a Hess girl. Samuel insisted that Gabriel return to the settlement, and Christian Wenger pled with him not to go. Gabriel left, hoping that he could return to the Wengers.

The following year Christopher Ulrich and Bright Star were married. Susanna missed her brothers badly and, following Christian's suggestion, she began to help Magdelena. Her loneliness was soon forgotten as she became busy helping other people.

Peter Miller and Conrad Weiser along with many others were baptized. Miller was a highly-educated minister from Berks County, Pennsylvania. He emphasized his break with the Reformed and Lutheran catechisms by burning his books. He spoke seven languages and would soon be director of printing and binding.

Michael Whitman, who was loyal to Britain and a member of the Reformed Church, moved next to the settlement. He opposed German printing in English territory. It is recorded that his teenage son threw stones at Miller and said, "So this is how they treat you, Brother Miller. They make you push a cart just like an animal."

Miller quietly went on moving his precious pulp that would become paper.

Weiser was an important government man in Penn's Woods. News of these baptisms reached back to Europe and people grew very angry at Beissel. No longer was it safe for a Father of the Desert to walk the road.

At that time, the solitary brethren had finished a place called Kedar, where they had their love feasts. They held midnight watches there, believing that at that hour God, the Judge, was expected to return. After four hours, the meeting ended and everyone went to work.

In Kedar, cells for the sisters were upstairs; cells for the brethren were down below. The conduct of these young people who came to live in celibacy was a reproach to the settlement. The Fathers of the Desert wanted to stay out of danger by removing the sisters; Beissel wanted to keep them together.

Although Beissel did not want wagons at the settlement, after much persuasion, the Eckerlins built wagons to aid in the building of Kedar. Once the building was finished, they secretly planned to bring business to the settlement. Beissel now knew that Israel's loyalty was now with his brothers rather than with him and his simple lifestyle. Yet Israel and Gabriel were Beissel's favored young men. He allowed them to furnish their cabin in luxury. There, guests received care, which caused envy among the others.

Emanuel was made an elder in another area. Born a priest and endowed with spiritual perversion, he was baptized for his mother in order to satisfy her spirit. People did not go along with such perversion and soon turned against him.

After the dignitaries' baptism, Beissel sent twelve fathers throughout Penn's Woods, as far away as New Jersey. Traveling barefoot, each carried a staff. Conrad Weiser's beard was so long that his former friends hardly recognized him. Government and religious leaders marveled that such respectable men would allow themselves to be governed by a man as despised as Beissel.

On the way, Marie Sauer and Elizabeth Wenger visited Magdelena. After their return, all the celibate men and women who were scattered throughout the country moved to the settlement. They used canes and walked barefooted. Elizabeth coughed constantly. The Nageles and their son made staffs for themselves and walked by the Wengers. They exchanged properties with the Kraybills, Eve's parents, who lived close to the settlement. Thus, this holy mode of a solitary life was put to an end in Penn's Woods. Rather than living as hermits, they lived in the convent.

After Conrad Weiser left his government position and no longer acted as interpreter, Penn's Woods could no longer wage war with the Indians or make peace with them. Only Weiser was able to converse with the Indians so that peace could prevail. Along with twenty horses, the governor visited the settlement, bringing along many others from Virginia and Maryland. Beissel and Maria Eicher—Mother Superior—held themselves aloof. The governor, hoping to gain Weiser, declared that he was well impressed with the place. Weiser, impressed with the governor, was offered the office of Justice of Peace. The convent was opposed, but Beissel thought it was of the Lord. Weiser received the office.

Beissel expected God to show favor toward them through Weiser, but as Weiser returned to his government work, he remembered Beissel's powers. Beissel had powers that even the government didn't have. Weiser wanted to catch Beissel and tell him that his powers were limited.

More settlers kept coming from other places to Beissel's settlement, but just as many moved away. Those who left found themselves in all kinds of trouble. It was impressed upon them that judgment would follow. Some became sick; a few died; and some lost their minds.

Hans Graf's son, David, came back from studying medicine in Germantown. His wife had died, which left him free to help Magdelena and Susanna. With the help of David Graf and Deacon Martin Graf, demons were cast out. People began to realize that when the true God was in control, satanic powers would flee.

Problems were undermining the settlement. When Beissel made Maria, the younger Eicher girl, a prioress, her older sister, Anna, became envious. Anna had asked Beissel to marry her, or at least giver her his name, but he refused.

All this made Anna quite angry with Beissel. Soon Weiser, the Justice of the Peace, received a report that Beissel and Anna had done away with a bastard child. This had been in court before and thrown out because of lack of evidence. Now Anna confessed the matter before Weiser in the presence of a housefather. Soon after that, Anna heard that her life was in danger.

Weiser, determined to catch Beissel, had another trial in Lancaster. At that trial, Anna took back what she had reported. She confessed that she made the charge because of envy. This report spread everywhere. The people were angry because Beissel again had worked his way out of trouble.

☩   ☩   ☩   ☩

One evening, Magdelena and Susanna were called to the home of Anna Eicher and her husband, whom she had married earlier in the day. Marie Sauer received them at the door, saying that she had come to help Anna.

"I am Anna's close friend," said Marie, "but no one must ever learn that I was here to help her. I leave her in your hands and in the hands of David Graf and your deacon, Brother Martin. You will soon observe, as I have, that Anna has been poisoned. Please free me of anything concerning this, and may God bless anything you do."

"You are free, Marie. I understand," Magdelena assured her. "No word of your presence shall leave this house."

Anna was already confused. Susanna quickly did everything she was told. Anna would die if she didn't get help.

When David and Martin arrived, Anna was unconscious. Though the men prayed for her healing, God chose to take her.

Anna's husband reported to them what had happened:

"After the trial in Lancaster, Anna left the settlement because she felt that her life was in danger. Today she returned home to her parents who owned land next to the first cabin built for the sisters. Some solitary sisters were there who appeared unfriendly. After Anna ate dinner with her parents, the sisters left, saying something about God's judgment being on her marriage. I met her at her parents' house, and this afternoon we were married. When we were ready to retire for the night, she became sick. She suspected that someone had put poison in her food. Should I report this to Weiser?"

"Go ahead, if you want your own life to be in danger," Martin replied. "Beissel will not be overcome." After they emptied every container of food in the house and comforted her husband, they left.

On the way home Martin told them Weiser's story. "After Weiser left his wife to live in celibacy, he became guilty of adultery. Weiser, who confessed this sin to Beissel and had Beissel pray for him, considered that was sufficient. The girl, who also bore the guilt, was re-baptized, and she and Weiser no longer had contact.

"Weiser knows that the civil law would punish adultery severely, but Beissel keeps them from it," Martin spoke rapidly. "He writes bills of divorcement, which even the law cannot write. One man, whose wife chose celibacy, took his neighbor as his wife and they lived in adultery.

"At the recent trial, Weiser hoped that Anna would help him catch Beissel, but again, Beissel skipped away. Anna's husband is a witness to Beissel's guilt, but testifying might cost him his life."

"Did Beissel leave the German Baptists so that he could hide his sin?" Magdelena asked.

"His choosing a life of celibacy in the den of serpents certainly put him out of existence for awhile," David suggested. "Back there he thought he could disobey the laws, such as working on Sunday, and after a time, his dealings with Anna Eicher would be forgotten."

"And, once more the people followed him, even the Eicher girls, and he felt compelled to allow them to come," Magdelena offered. "Surely that would hide his sins even better."

"It might look that way, but we are surmising," Brother Martin cautioned.

"Perhaps we'd better let God expose Beissel's sins," Magdelena agreed. "Our hands are full enough with taking care of the problems Beissel has made."

"Beissel's demonic powers have his followers communing with the spirits of the dead. Christopher Sauer says that he talked with the dead when he visited his wife. He can witness to that," Martin declared with certainty.

"Some houses rattle at night, and the demons make so much disturbance that the people can't sleep. One righteous man didn't believe this was true; however, after spending the night in one of these houses, he was grateful to return to his own bed the next night.

"Others are plagued by the devil pulling off their shoes, stockings, even their dresses or pants. It even happens in public. Only after the spiritual brethren cast out the demons is there release.

"This afternoon Christian told me that his sister Elizabeth died at the settlement yesterday," Martin informed them. "Though they were invited to the funeral, they couldn't make themselves go."

Susanna longed for the day when the Conestoga Valley would be rid of such things.

"The Eckerlins and Nageles are the only Mennonites who with remain with Beissel. I pray daily that they might exchange the strange powers lurking about the Conestoga Valley for the power of God," Martin concluded.

Chapter 34

Overcome Evil With Good

It was the cold winter of 1747. So much had happened in the recent years.

As Susanna went out for a last armful of wood before dark, the smell of smoke in the air warned her that something was burning. She hoped that David would soon be home.

> Susanna hadn't been surprised when Deacon Martin Graf had visited her and Magdelena, asking if she would consider marrying David Graf. She had no doubt that God was in it, but only after gaining the approval of Christian Wenger and Grandfather Huber did she say yes. Now, after ten years of marriage, their home was blessed with three children.
>
> Magdelena, who lived a short distance from them, was close enough that the three of them could work together when medical help was needed.
>
> At last Marie Sauer was safe with her husband. Finally, their son had persuaded Marie to return to Christopher.
>
> Jacob Eberly had proved himself long enough. Maria Huber married him.
>
> Four years earlier, Beissel had made Israel Eckerlin a prior. The Eckerlins had selfishly claimed that office as long as possible. Perhaps the problem was jealousy of the celibate brethren; or, maybe it was Maria Eicher's hatred for Beissel and anyone who held the office of prior. It may also have been the Eckerlins' craving for leadership. Susanna was not sure why, but the Eckerlins were not looked upon favorably.

Israel's term as prior lasted four years, ending two years ago on September 4, 1745. His younger brother Gabriel took his place while Samuel and Israel headed west, over the Allegheny Mountains, to French and Indian country. The fourth brother, Emanuel, joined the German Baptists in Germantown.

Gabriel unknowingly ruled his young men as selfishly as Israel had done. The household broke up, and Gabriel made arrangements to return to the Wengers. In the mean time, Samuel arrived and took Gabriel west with him.

The settlement was relieved to be rid of the Eckerlins. Everyone could finally do as he pleased. Underhandedly, Maria Eicher turned those who chose to live the solitary lifestyle against Israel, which left the settlement in turmoil. Beissel, knowing her intentions, went to great measures to spare Israel, but to no avail.

After Beissel told those who were inclined to go to leave, many left that very night. The thriving business activity of the settlement ended, much to the Philadelphia merchants' disappointment.

David arrived home with an armful of wood and hurried out for more. Susanna fingered the Bible, which they had purchased from Christopher Sauer before his wife returned home. It was the first Bible printed in a European language on American soil. David and Susanna felt privileged to have a Bible in their home.

Susanna and David had also rejoiced when their leaders asked Peter Miller to translate the Martyrs Mirror *from Holland Dutch to German. The settlement had the only printing press in America that could do it, and who other than Peter Miller could do the translating?*

The Mennonites said that after it was proven to be doctrinally safe, they would buy it. Two Mennonite brethren from the east lived at the settlement, checking each page as it was printed. These breth-

ren also enjoyed the beautiful four-part singing at midnight. Especially touching was the hymn, "A Mighty Fortress Is Our God."

Finally, David was satisfied that there was enough wood for the night. He faced Susanna, ready to talk.

"Why is the air smoky?" Susanna asked.

"Last night the Eckerlin mill burned to the ground," David informed her.

"No!" Susanna replied in shock. "Their mill was full of grain. Did they save the grain?"

"No," David answered. "Last night, when everyone was in a sound sleep, the miller discovered the fire. It was one of the coldest nights, yet those in the settlement tried to quench the flames, but to no avail. They did extinguish a wall of burning logs to keep the fire from spreading. They also saved the sawmill, which had started to burn."

"Was the paper mill saved?" Susanna cried. "It was so close to the flour mill."

"God spared that," David said solemnly. "The paper to be used for printing the *Martyrs Mirror* was saved; but they can't do printing without eating. Within four hours, the whole flour mill, three stones, and much wheat was consumed. Those stones which Samuel shaped in the oil mill are gone. There are no other stones like them in America. A large quantity of oil and 500 bushels of flax seed were lost, too. Samuel's complete fulling mill, and all that belonged to it, are gone.

"Thus, God has permitted all the mammon, which the Eckerlins have gained by scraping and miserly conduct, to be destroyed. The settlement has enough food to last for eight days. Today, Beissel began to appeal to God. This moved the fathers to hold a conference. Every householder willingly sacrificed all they could spare for those in the settlement. Even this was not enough, so they bought enough to last until the mill can be rebuilt."

"Don't we Mennonites owe them anything?" Susanna suggested. "They still accuse us low-down Mennonites of starting that fire fifteen years ago. We still hold a grudge against Beissel for taking our preacher and young people. Maybe we weren't prepared as well as we should have been to keep them. Can't we forgive and help them build their mill?

"The Bible says in Romans 12:20-21, 'If thine enemy hunger, feed him; if he thirst, give him drink: for in so doing thou shalt heap coals of fire on his head. Be not overcome of evil, but overcome evil with good.'"

"Remember the vengeance those who left to live in solitude had against the Eckerlin Regime after they left?" David reminded Susanna. "In one night they uprooted the 1,000 fruit trees which the Eckerlins had planted. They sold the Eckerlins' Babylon-like bell to the Reformed and Lutheran congregations in Lancaster, and zealously tore down the spire.

This 1749 Martyrs Mirror *owned by Johannes Jacob Huber, son of Hans Huber who arrived at Graf's Run about the same time as Hans Groff along with the Bear, Baer, Bar family is lying open on the 1819* zappetisch *(farmers table) used as a lecturn until a pulpit was installed at Hammer Creek Mennonite Church. Christian Bomberger undoubtedly stood behind this lecturn to preach as well as visiting Bishop Peter Eby, Benjamin Eby, and Jacob Zimmerman. The small book in the background is Hans Graf's* Ausbund, *and the larger book which it sits on is a Froschauer Bible brought from Switzerland. (Muddy Creek Farm Library)*

"The common wash house was burned down at night because it was used by their young people for courting. I hardly know how that could have been blamed on the Eckerlins. The Eckerlins had placed the brethren's house so that a hill separated them and the sisters' area. Now the brethren's house, which is large enough to accommodate 100 men, is in the area where the trees were uprooted. It is close enough to the sisters' house that they can carry on a conversation between them.

"Their new prior has put them to work. I can't imagine where they're getting the money. Beissel has a new cabin, and the chapel and meeting hall is ornate, with Gothic letters, a gallery, and a hall for the love feasts. Their are no other buildings in North America that are so durably built.

"If God is punishing them for what they did to the Eckerlins, should we help them?" David reasoned. "Neither can I bear the thought of their tonsure. Every female and male has their hair shaved, even though they know the Scriptures teach differently. Beissel says it is of the Lord. Can we help such people, yet still not condone their actions?"

"Is it not our Christian duty to help them in spite of everything?" Susanna insisted.

"I hope every Mennonite brother will lay all his doubts aside and think like you," David exclaimed. "I agree this is our time to heap coals of fire on their heads."

☩　☩　☩　☩

During the coldest season of the year, in six weeks time, the whole community of Mennonites, Lutherans, German Baptists, and Indians had placed one set of millstones in operation. Everyone contributed wood, or whatever he could, and helped with his team.

In December 1748, Peter Miller visited David and Susanna when he delivered to Christian Wenger and each of the Grafs their precious *Martyrs Mirror*.

It had taken three years to print these books. Surprisingly, during that time, Beissel had every member of the convent under strict discipline. Each did his work at his place and on time. There was a solemnness among them as they read about the awful persecutions and deaths of the Anabaptists.

David and Susanna received their copy with thankful hearts. Now they had three precious books of their own: a Bible, a *Martyrs Mirror*, and an *Ausbund*. Peter Miller was satisfied that, with his completed work, the rift between the Mennonites and Beissel was lifted. He, too, had overcome evil with good.

Calliography artist Abram Kurtz of the Ephrata Cloisters penned this page in the 1749 Martyrs Mirror *in 1757 for Johannes Jacob Huber, son of Immigrant Hans Huber. The verse underneath his name is Psalm 15:1-2: "Lord, who shall abide in thy tabernacle? Who shall stand in thy holy hill? He that walketh uprightly." (Muddy Creek Farm Library)*

Chapter 35

Captive

Israel began sending letters to Beissel to be read to those living a solitary life. However, Beissel refused to read more than one of these long, railing letters.

In 1760, Samuel and Gabriel tried to return to the settlement. While there, Gabriel visited the Wengers and planned to return to their home to stay. He was a miserable man, wanting to free himself from Israel.

Soon after that, Israel manipulated them away from the settlement on business. Then he tried to return by himself. The brethren received him graciously; however, when they saw the "old" Israel spirit desiring to rule, they refused him, asking him to move to a cabin by himself at the edge of the settlement. In anger, he ran away and waited for his brothers' return to Ephrata. They found Israel and were forced to accompany him home to stay. Again Gabriel was made captive.

Later, Samuel took a fifty-sheet letter to Beissel, who refused it. Samuel went on to Germantown, letting all know that the Eckerlins had left Beissel for good.

David and Susanna were happy with their congregation on Graf's Run. Grandfather and Grandmother Huber and Magdelena and Hans Graf had passed on. Deacon Martin Graf and the Graf brothers took it upon themselves to build the Groffdale Mennonite Meetinghouse.

The churches were growing. Christian's preaching circuit included Metzlers, Carpenters, and Groffdale. Children were marrying and raising Mennonite families around Beissel's settlement in the town of Ephrata.

Still, those living the solitary life had trouble. Christopher Sauer made it known that the number 666, the mark of the beast, was found in Beissel's name.

Maria Eicher still disliked Beissel for putting her younger sister in charge of the women's area at the settlement. Recently, another of her sisters at the settlement was blessed with triplets. The following morning, she and the father of the babies, Hans Nagele's son, were forced to leave and get married. All this increased Maria's hatred for Beissel.

Maria did not allow Beissel in the sisters' area and determined to get rid of every prior that he hired. After a futile attempt to remove the women's area from under Beissel's care, she remained content to have the sisters' worship service separate.

In 1767 the news arrived that Israel and Gabriel had been taken captive by the French. "Where is Samuel?" David and Susanna wondered as they lifted them daily to the throne of grace. How relieved Susanna was that she had forgiven Samuel.

This medicine recipe book owned by Dr. Christian Weber was copied in 1833 by Dr. Graf—the grandson of Hans' grandson. (Muddy Creek Farm Library)

CHAPTER 36

This Elysian Dale

Susanna, having passed her fifty-fourth birthday in November, sat with David in their small kitchen. Their family was grown and their last child had just left home. Samuel Eckerlin sat across the table from them, his aging face lined with distress, and his shoulders drooped in discouragement. He was sorrowful about something, and David and Susanna were waiting for him to talk.

> *Three years earlier, in 1765, Samuel had returned to Ephrata a broken man. No one knew what happened to Israel and Gabriel. Samuel never mentioned what happened. Emanuel had started a*

German Baptist congregation in Georgia which no one knew much about.
"Someday, Samuel will tell us the story," David had assured Susanna. "Now, it is too painful to share."
Samuel had not gone back with Beissel. Since he practiced medicine, he and David had books of medicine recipes, bottles full of medicine, and the blood-letting page in Christopher Sauer's Almanac in common.
Johannes Landis had died in a realm of spiritual darkness with a despairing fear that his wife would leave him. He refused to forgive Beissel until the end. After Johannes's death, his wife entered the solitary life.
At least Samuel was not in a realm of darkness. He was grieving, but he still trusted in God.
On December 24, Maria Eicher died. She had held a hatred toward Beissel until the very end.
Beissel also had died six months ago, with the brethren crowding around him and the sisters standing on benches behind them. They had expected he would struggle with demons, but he died calmly.
Peter Miller became superintendent. He didn't have visions, but he seemed interested in helping others. David predicted that in a short time the settlement for those choosing the celibate life would come to an end. Too many kept leaving and joining other religious groups.

"I've received news about Gabriel and Israel," Samuel began, immediately causing David's and Susanna's attention to turn toward him. "They died ten years ago in France where our father died," Samuel cried. Drying his tears, he went on. "After their capture, the Indians mercilessly skinned parts of their cheeks as they cut off their beards, using tomahawks to drive them like animals through the snow-covered mountains.
"Gabriel and Israel, sold as spies to the French, moved to Montreal and then to Quebec. Though food was scarce, they were

allowed to beg for food, thus becoming objects of pity. Along with other prisoners, they were transported to France. Due to the lack of food and the torture, they became frustrated and unable to control their tempers.

"When Israel knew that he soon would die, he became a m ember of an order of monks in the Roman Church. He always had a peculiar esteem for friars. There they gave him tonsure and called him bon Chretien. I fear for his soul.

"With the help of an Anabaptist prisoner, Gabriel gladly committed his life to God. He regretted that he had left the Wengers against the wishes of his mother and other Mennonites.

"I should have helped Gabriel return to the Wengers," Samuel cried. "Israel ruled all of us to his own and our destruction." As Samuel wept, Susanna and David wept with him.

Gabriel is gone, Susanna cried within. *Peter and Christopher and their families have moved west of the Susquehanna with Peter Grafs. Only we, along with Christians, remain to care. Through friendship with my dear husband, Samuel has returned.*

When Samuel gained control of himself, David asked, "Where is Emanuel?"

"He died soon after he went to Georgia. His congregation was not impressed with him. He told them that if they would not respect his leadership, he would die—and he died. That is all I know."

"And that leaves you alone," David spoke with sympathy.

"Yes, I am alone. I've come to Ephrata to help others who have become confused with Beissel's false doctrine, but I'm confused and sorrowing myself."

"Where did you go after you left Beissel?" David asked.

"Israel was in the height of bitterness, and we almost ran after him to our home west of the Alleghenies. Some of the celibate brethren followed and pled with us to come back. Israel refused and threatened to have nothing more to do with us if we returned. We settled at a place where the Indians could protect us from the French. There we lost all desire for Sabbath meetings, communion, baptism, and righteous living. We became free thinkers as money flowed freely into our pockets. We lived in a luxurious house and had servants and horses. In the meantime, Israel, still seething with revenge, railed upon

Beissel and the celibate in more lengthy letters. I never told him that they read the first letter, but refused the rest.

"I also became angry with Beissel. Daily Gabriel went hunting to get away from our terrible conversations. He learned that Beissel considered hunting improper for a Christian, and he doubted that Christian would approve of it either. Had I not brought him back to Ephrata, he would have gone insane with continuous crying.

"Israel crushed Gabriel's and my desire to stay at Ephrata again and again. We feared him while he led us like lambs to the slaughter back to our home in the west. Gabriel and I began visiting the Mennonites in Virginia. Our hearts returned to the Mennonite faith. I considered marrying a Mennonite girl when new trouble began.

"A warning came that we were no longer safe from the enemy Indians and the French. Israel would not hear of it. To satisfy him, I went to Virginia to obtain rights to live in the west. Secretly, I hoped that the government men would convince him that it was not safe.

"Back home, in the meantime, the servant had warned Israel of the enemy at their door. Israel continued to write his accusing letters to Beissel, paying no heed. The Indians burned our home to the ground, taking my brothers, our servant, and our horses.

"The soldiers of the Virginia government and I came upon our home as the last of the embers were burning. An enemy Indian remained to kill anyone who would try to follow them. The soldier who was hiding said that he was ready to kill me when he saw me weeping. As he watched, his heart softened. Slowly he went after his companions.

"We had no idea if my brothers were captured or burned in the fire, but we saw the horses' tracks. That was in 1757. They died in 1758."

"And now, in 1768, you've learned what happened," David comforted Samuel. "Today is your day of sorrow, and we are sorrowing with you."

"I've come for another reason," Samuel said after their tears dried. "Yesterday Marie Eicher died, taking her intense hatred for Beissel with her. Later, she was mocked when she was found mourning at his graveside. A friend kept Marie's money for the day when she planned to leave the settlement. Marie never found a better way than to hate."

There was silence. Susanna guessed what Samuel wanted. She waited.

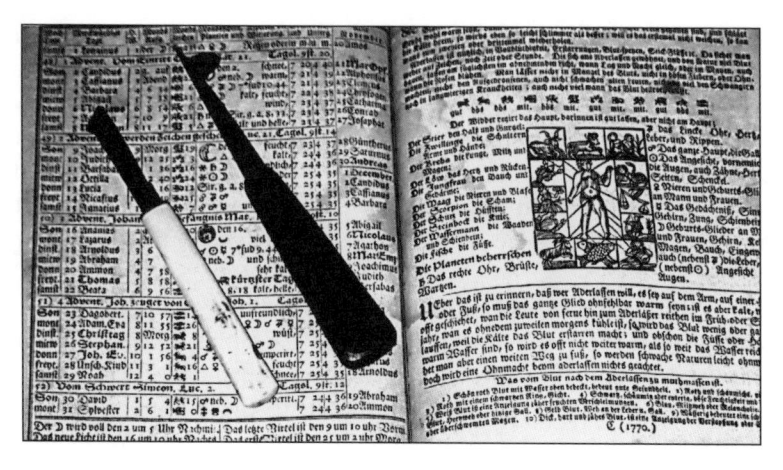

The right page is the blood letting page of Christopher Sauer's Almanac. *The first edition of this* Almanac *was first printed in 1738 with this particular page appearing in all editions. Also, pictured are two blood-letting knives frequently used in days gone by. (Muddy Creek Farm Library)*

"Susanna, I do not want you to hate me because I caused your sister to do wrong," Samuel's voice trembled. "That is no way to die. I take all the blame myself for Catherine's leaving. She wanted to stay with me when I was taken up with Israel's notions; and, she never betrayed me, but rather chose to take the blame herself for her actions. Marie Sauer scolded me many times for what I did to Catherine. What could I do? I loved Catherine. I was going against my mother's wishes. My father would have never agreed with my actions, but I lacked control over myself and continued to follow Israel. I am sorry, Susanna. Please forgive me," he pled.

"I'll gladly forgive you. Actually, I've forgiven you long ago," Susanna assured him. "David and I have been praying for you."

"And I know that God is willing to forgive you, too," David comforted him.

"If only I had followed my mother's and church leader's advice, I would not have failed," Samuel wept in remorse. "Instead, I could have been a help to my brothers and to Catherine."

"You need to forgive yourself," David reminded Samuel. "Only in doing that will you find rest."

They sat a long time in silence. Samuel gave David a letter edged in black. "Sometime you may read about Israel's and Gabriel's end," he said painfully.

"Will you forgive yourself and enjoy life from here on?" David begged. "Experience gives us wisdom to understand others. God has work for you, Samuel. Come back to the church and find help from the brethren. The security that we feel in our brotherhood makes our life a bit of heaven right here in the Conestoga Valley."

"With God's help and yours, I want to do all you have said," Samuel promised as he grasped David's hand. "Thank you. Pray for me."

Susanna recalled the lovely cabin and barn that Hans Graf had built for his first wife. These were only a few of the gracious deeds he had done for Magdelena—his first love. And how he loved the maid who had become his second wife and given him both joy and more children. Hans loved both of his wives, but he loved God and his church also, and remained pure, free, and noble to the end.

He loved the following song: *"Meine zufriedenheit, was ich nicht ändern kann nehm ich geduldig an."* (My total peace rests in satisfaction; what I cannot change, I will endure patiently.)

Hans had found his elysian dale. She, Susuanna, had found her bit of heaven too. Oh, that Samuel would find a bit of heaven on the Conestoga also.

"Sometime you may read about Israel's and Gabriel's end," he said painfully. (Muddy Creek Farm Library)

This beautiful barn was built by Hans Graf about 1720. It was large enough to sufficiently supply the needs of his family and is an excellent model of a barn built at that time. Located along Farmersville Road down over the hill just a few feet from what is now the entrance to Fairmount Homes Retirement Community (the old building) at Farmersville, Lancaster County, Pennsylvania. The hump in the road and in the land beyond the barn, and the trees in front of the barn remain today. The cabin that Hans Graf built for his first wife was located slightly to the left and above the barn, providing a spectacular view of the area around Graf's Run. This photograph was taken July 1963 before the barn was torn down. (Muddy Creek Farm Library)

Bibliography

Durnbaugh, Donald, *The Brethren Encyclopedia*.
Gilbert, Russel Wieder. *A Picture of the Pennsylvania Germans*. Pennsylvania Historical Association, 1962.
Heincke, Milton. *History of Ephrata*. Historical Society of the Cocalico Valley, 1974.
Lamech & Agrippa. *Chronican Ephratense*, New York: Lenox Hill, 1889, reprinted 1972. A History of the Community of the Seventh Day Baptists at Ephrata, Lancaster Co., Pa.; translated by J. Max Hark, D.D., Burt Franklin, N.Y.
Longenecker, Stephen L. *The Christopher Sauers*. Elgin, Ill.: The Brethren Press, 1981.
Sangmeister, Ezechiel. *Journal of the Historical Society of the Cocalico Valley*, Vol. IV. 1992.
Sloane, Eric. *Diary of an Early American Boy—Noah Blake, 1805*. Wilfred Funk, Inc., 1965.
Spohn, Clarence E. *The Eicher Family and Their Homestead*. Ephrata, Pa.: Eicher Arts Center, 1995.
The Three Earls. New Holland, Pa.: Rank & Sandoe, 1876. Proceedings of the Centennial Jubilee, New Holland, Pa., July 4, 1876.
Ward, Mary Francis. *Fast as the Wind*. 1978.
Wenger, A. Grace. *275th Anniversary of the Groffdale Mennonite Church*. 1992.

Other Sources

Clarence Spohn, historian and writer at the Ephrata Cloister, offered much insight into the tenor of thought from 1725 to 1735.

A visit to the Hans Herr House with farmer Donald Herr who remembered the state of the house before it was renovated was profitable.

Informative visits to and from Amos B. Hoover and his wife, Nora, and the opportunity to photograph some of his collection from the Muddy Creek Farm Library.

Information from my late mother-in-law Esther Zook, who remembered in detail how things were done in earlier days, was very helpful.

Other information was given verbally by various descendants of Hans Graf who are interested in history. Information, which seems to be accurate, was passed down from one who heard it from the Graf family. I don't believe this information is recorded in writing.

I made numerous visits to the following: Ephrata Cloister; buildings that remain in the Graf's Run area; Peter Graf's mill; Theodorus Eby's house; Bitzer's (Fiandt's) Mill; Eberly's Covered Bridge; Long's barn; the site of Hans Graf's Mill; the Eberly Graveyard; and possible dwelling site in Indiantown. Millway (where the Hammer Creek and Middle Creek flowed into the Cocalico Creek) is where my grandparents, Benjamin Eberly and Annie Oberholtzer, raised their family of ten.

Also, the site of Fairmount Homes Retirement Community (on top of Cat's Back) is inspiring. As we visit my mother, Anna Mary Eberly Martin Weaver, who lives there, I've tried to see it as Susanna saw it amid the forest-clad Conestoga Valley.

Graf's Spring, the Christian Wenger farm, Hans Nagele farm, the site of Hans Graf's second home, and Cooper's Blacksmith (which they say was built by Marx Graf) are refreshing places to see.

When I was an infant, a black friend of my father, Paul Martin (now deceased), risked his life to stop a runaway car in which I was riding. My father taught a Sunday School class at Welsh Mountain Mission home. He loved and was loved by the black people, and I attribute my love to help black people and show respect to them for what one of them did for me.

As a child and youth in the Lancaster Conference Groffdale Mennonite Church and a resident of New Holland, a mile from where the Hubers had lived, I never dreamed of the trials and victories our forefathers experienced during their first years on the Conestoga Creek and Mill Creek. It inspires me to pass on to our descendants the faith that has been passed on to me.

> *O for a faith that will not shrink*
> *Though pressed by many a foe,*
> *That will not tremble on the brink*
> *Of any earthly woe.*
> *That will not murmur nor complain*
> *Beneath the chastening rod,*
> *But in the hour of grief or pain*
> *Can lean upon its God.*
> *A faith that keeps the narrow way*
> *Till life's last spark is fled,*
> *And with a pure and heav'nly ray*
> *Lights up a dying bed.*
> *Lord, give me such a faith as this,*
> *And then, whate'er may come,*
> *I'll taste e'en here the hallowed bliss*
> *Of an eternal home. Amen.*

(Written by William H. Bathurst, 1831, *Church Hymnal*. Scottdale, Pa.: Mennonite Publishing House, 1927.)